Come On Philly, We Can Do Better.

Come On Philly, We Can Do Better.

Julius A Williams III

Authentic Publishing LLC

COME ON PHILLY, WE CAN DO BETTER. Copyright © 2009 by Julius A. Williams III. All rights reserved. Printed in the United States of America. No part of this book may be used or reproduced in any manner whatsoever without written permission except in the case of brief quotations embodied in critical articles or reviews. For information, address Authentic Publishing LLC, P.O. Box 8486, Philadelphia, Pennsylvania 19101.

www.AuthenticPublishingLLC.com

Authentic Publishing LLC books may be purchased for business or educational use. For information, please write to Authentic Publishing LLC at the above address, or contact Authentic Publishing LLC through the above website.

ISBN 978-0-9843577-0-3

FIRST EDITION

The stories in this book are based on things I saw and heard, and on things told to me, during my time at a Philadelphia public middle school. Events are sometimes relayed out of actual chronological order. Conversations are not relayed verbatim and are in some instances combined or condensed.

Contents

Before Parish Hill   1

Welcome to Parish Hill   3

Tyreak   6

Demetrius White   12

Kushner and Leslie   19

Tested   26

Kushner's Fall   32

A Nightmare for Ms. Leslie   34

Marlow   41

Ellway Joins the 'Oh No!'s   50

Lakara   52

Chafie Fields   65

Still Going   78

School Police Office   88

Months Later   96

The Next Day in the Grievance Center   106

Years Later   117

Before Parish Hill

I accepted the job over the phone. The Philadelphia school district had offered it eagerly, desperate for anyone to fill the spot, and I was the brave fool who was willing. I was not told that it would be challenging, which would have been an understatement. Nor was I told of any special circumstances, a warning that still would not have prepared me for what I would encounter at Parish Hill. In fact, all the school district operator told me was the location of the school, who I was replacing, and for how long – which turned out to be wrong.

The operator said I would be filling in for the guidance counselor, who was taking a ten-day leave, but when I arrived, I learned I would be filling the position for the remainder of the school year. It was October. The incidents that took place and the characters I encountered during that year were like nothing I had ever seen before. I wrote them down as I saw or heard them, using any free time I was blessed with to write.

So this isn't a story, it's an account of my experiences over those many months. As confusing and disturbing as it may seem, this book offers a glimpse of what the school was all about. Names and identifying information have been changed to protect the innocent – and not so innocent.

Welcome to Parish Hill

"Fuck you, you fat bitch! You ain't shit. You ain't nothin' but a stupid fat bitch!" These were the ugly harsh words that flowed from one mother to another as I entered Parish Hill on my first day.

Ms. Whitney, Clarice Whitney's mother, stood in front of the main office ranting. Willy Reeves, the hall monitor, and I stood in front of the office's glass doors to stop Ms. Whitney and Clarice's grandmother from getting at their prize inside the office – Shaena Brown and her mother. Shaena and her mother were both large women of great strength, and they were using that strength on Officer Ellway and Officer Travis, our school police officers, who were having the damnedest time keeping them inside the office.

"Oh, hell no, hell no! No one is going to talk to my mother that way!" Shaena shouted as she huffed and puffed and gave another go at bulldozing over the school police.

As she charged, the officers caught her, and their backs slammed into the door causing it to shake and rattle. The door was locked, so it couldn't open, but the force made dust and woodchips fly from the doorframe and trickle to the floor.

"Yeah, that's right, come on out. Come out here, and get your ass whipped, you fat bitch," Ms. Whitney said as she removed both earrings and one of her shoes, ready to use the high heel as a weapon.

I glanced inside the office, where I saw the principal, Mrs. Matthews, and the office secretaries hiding under their desks. Principal Matthews peeked her head around a corner of her desk. I would later hear from staff that principal Matthews kept a close watch on these types of incidents – not to assist, but to write-up any staff misconduct.

Shaena's mother made another charge. She knocked Officer Ellway to the floor, sandwiching Officer Travis between her and the door. She followed the charge with a punch at the glass.

Ms. Whitney immediately countered from outside the office with a heel to the same spot on the window.

"Ten-four, ten-four! It's pandemonium up here! We need backup—now! Now, damn it! Now!" Ellway yelled into his walkie as he lay on the ground. "Can anyone hear me?" Ellway called again. "Can anyone hear me?" He was hoping that his friend and fellow cop, Officer Cleveland, who worked at a neighboring school, would come to our aid. He did, but by the time he arrived, all the ruckus had stopped.

Shaena and her mother left the school quietly after Shaena convinced her mother that it was time to go. They walked right out of the school – no one said anything to them. Officer Cleveland went into the office to talk to principal Matthews.

Ms. Whitney, Clarice, and Grandma Whitney did not go so calmly. Ms. Whitney spent a few minutes mumbling to herself, shouted a few more choice words, and then said goodbye in her own way: "This school is a piece of shit. A joke—a fucking joke," she shouted. "You got that bullshit-ass principal, bullshit teachers, and those plastic, fake, toy-cop ass school police."

"Hey, miss, you better watch who you are talking to like that or I'll—" Officer Ellway said, walking over to Ms. Whitney with a slight limp from being thrust to the ground earlier.

"Or you'll what?" Ms. Whitney asked, ready for action.

"Ellway, relax. It's not even worth it," Officer Travis said as he stepped between Officer Ellway and Ms. Whitney and placed his hands on Ellway's shoulders.

"Yeah, that's what I thought. Come on, Clarice, let's go."

Officer Cleveland came out of the office shaking his head. "She's not pressing any charges. Let's go, boys," he said to the officers he'd brought over for backup.

This incident came to represent what Parish Hill Middle School was all about – children *and* adults acting out of order, a school staff that was helpless to stop it, and an administration that was unwilling to stop it.

Tyreak

"Stop turning my doorknob," I said.

"What?"

"Stop turning my doorknob. I know you're turning my doorknob because you're trying to find out if it's open so you can go in and take something when I'm not there."

"If I wanted to take something out of your office, I would break in there."

"Shut up and go to class."

"No. You go to your office."

I had this argument with Tyreak Jones, a 16-year-old seventh grader. After he told me to "go to my office," he ran down the hallway. It took all the strength I had not to run down the hallway after him and treat him like he was a grown man.

Tyreak would have deserved it. He was a troublemaker. Anything he was supposed to do was never done. He never went to class. When Tyreak was in a classroom, it was never the class he was supposed to be in. He would just waltz into a classroom like he belonged there. When questioned by a teacher or asked to leave, he would start arguing with the teacher – just like he started arguing with me outside my office. It was almost as if his sole purpose was to come to school to start trouble.

"Move out of my way, Tyreak. I am so sick of this," Ms. Wilson said as she threw her hands above her head in frustration.

Tyreak had entered her class as he often did – without permission and with the intent to cause trouble and recruit other troublemakers. This time, he was blocking Ms. Wilson's way as she tried to get out of the room.

"Will you just move?" she asked.

"Shut up, bitch. I ain't goin' nowhere."

Ms. Wilson's eyes started to water. She reached for the phone next to the door to call for help. Tyreak blocked that as well.

"Just let me out of here!" Ms. Wilson shouted.

The class quieted. Tyreak moved to the side as if he was going to recruit help from the class, and Ms. Wilson stepped into the hallway.

There was no time left in the last period of the school day, and most of the children, including Tyreak, left the room and went home. Four or five students who felt bad for Ms. Wilson stayed after class and cleaned up her room as she sat crying at her desk.

I walked into her room to find out what had happened. She balled up her fist and widened her eyes as she told me the entire story. "He was everywhere. Running around the room, throwing paper, cursing at students, opening my desk drawers.

And then he wouldn't let me leave the room; he stood in front of the door and refused to let me out!"

Ms. Wilson shook a little as she spoke, and I could understand why. She had truly been frightened. Tyreak was only a seventh grader, but he was almost old enough to sign himself in and out of school. Ms. Wilson was right to be scared of him.

As she told her story, principal Matthews and two teachers from the third floor entered the room and sat down.

"What happened?" Matthews asked as she pulled out a pen and pad, acting as if she was concerned and was going to handle the situation right away. Ms. Wilson took a deep breath, looked out the window, and explained the whole incident again.

"Sounds like a criminal offense," Mr. Kushner yelled sarcastically from the back of the room where he was sitting.

Principal Matthews did not acknowledge Kushner's comment. "Ms. Wilson, Tyreak will be punished for his actions. You have every reason to be upset."

"But Mrs. Matthews, this isn't the first time he came into the room and acted up like this. He has been doing this all year. As a matter of fact, all three years, and nothing has been done. It's ridiculous! It's so hard to work like this. I'm sorry for being so upset."

"Please, Ms. Wilson, don't apologize. You're right, and Tyreak will be reprimanded." As principal Matthews spoke, the mood in the room was doubtful.

Principal Matthews was the only person in the school who could give Tyreak exactly what he needed – expulsion –but we all knew that nothing was going to happen to him.

Tyreak was suspended that day, but for something that had nothing to do with Ms. Wilson. He started a food fight in the cafeteria. Then, even though he was suspended, he was still in school because, as it was explained to me very nonchalantly by Ms. Gladstone, our vice principal, sending Tyreak to an empty home would have been a violation of district policy, or so it seemed. If Tyreak's mother new about the policy, when she was home, she probably wouldn't answer the phone.

Tyreak eventually served his suspension at home. Surprisingly, at the end of his suspension, his mother came to reinstate him. Though policy required it, Tyreak's mother had never been to school before to reinstate him after a suspension. Instead, the school had made a habit of doing it without her involvement.

That practice made no sense to me. The whole point of requiring parents to come to school was to emphasize their role in helping change the child's future behavior at the school. The parent had to take time off from work, or from whatever they were doing, but that reinforced the seriousness of the situation. So it seemed that the more out of line the child's behavior was, the more important it was to have the parent involved in the reinstatement.

This time, Tyreak's mother came to the school because Tyreak's suspension letter stated that Tyreak would not be allowed back into school without his mother present for a meeting. At that meeting, Ms. Gladstone was supposed to talk Tyreak's mother into signing a voluntary transfer form.

Many staff felt that given Tyreak's repeated suspensions and his mother's past failures to follow school policy on reinstatement, Principal Matthews could easily have stepped in, given Tyreak a disciplinary transfer form, and made him go to a reform school. That never happened, perhaps because of school district rules and regulations that had to be followed and complicated matters, or perhaps because of Principal Matthews' own decision that it not be done.

At first, I wondered why, but chatter among the staff quickly provided a possible explanation: Mrs. Matthews had a reputation for being money hungry and selfish. It was rumored that if she transferred too many students like Tyreak in one year, she would become ineligible for a bonus in her salary. So, the staff felt that she was looking out for her pockets instead of the students. I had no way of telling first hand whether the rumor was true, but it would explain why she tried to get Ms. Gladstone to convince Tyreak's mother to sign the voluntary transfer form.

After the meeting, everyone dispersed. Principal Matthews and I stood in the hallway. She was mumbling and looking at me out of the corner of her eye.

"Excuse me, Mrs. Matthews," I said, walking closer to her so I could hear what she was saying.

"If I were Ms. Wilson, I would have said, 'Okay, you're not going to move out of my way? All right, boop," she said, throwing a punch as if she would have hit Tyreak with a right cross. Her eyes were wide, searching for approval.

I just sighed and nodded my head. This was the reaction Mrs. Matthews usually received from the staff. She wanted us to believe she was tough and meant business, but if she was really about taking action, she would have already booped someone. She could have booped someone during any one of the many incidents she had witnessed or after one of the many times she had been disrespected.

I started to feel insulted. Was she trying to get me to do her dirty work by trying to convince me it was okay to boop one of the kids? Was she hinting that she would respect me more if I did? Whatever it was, I knew she would not be behind me if I was pushed to the edge by one of the students. She would write me up, press charges, and have me arrested as she had done with other staff members.

I also knew there was one kid she would not even think about booping. She knew this kid would boop her right back.

Demetrius White

As a counselor at the school, I didn't get a chance to deal with many students that behaved decently or had respectable grades. I wasn't fortunate enough to interact with that tiny group on a regular basis; I dealt with the students who had the most problems.

Demetrius White was one of those students. He didn't say much. He didn't do much either. But when he did do something, he did it to the best of his ability. And when he talked, he backed up his words with action.

"Hey, Mr. Williams."

"What's goin' on, Rocky?" That was the nickname I had given Demetrius because of all the stories I heard about his father being a well-known professional fighter. "Don't knock anyone out today, buddy."

"All right, Mr. Williams," he answered as he walked up the stairs to class. He had a devilish grin on his face as he usually did – as if he was up to something. If he was up to something, I, and the rest of the school, would find out about it shortly.

Come On Philly, We Can Do Better.

Being a man who grew up hearing all types of childhood menace stories from my father, who grew up in the city, I felt that Demetrius was the only child who made the stories come to life. Apparently, I wasn't the only person who thought so.

"Oh yeah, Demetrius White. That kid can fight. His father, Dominique White, can fight too," Officer Ellway said, while he, Officer Travis, and I sat in his office. I would go down there from time to time and sit in a chair on the other side of Ellway's desk. His desk was in one corner, and Travis' desk was in the other corner.

"Dominique White, the boxer?" I asked, raising my eyebrows.

"Yeah. This kid isn't like the rest of these punks in the school. He hits hard. I mean hard," Ellway said, his eyes widening in amazement. "One time he was angry with one of those teachers on the third floor, and he—"

"He hit the teacher?" I interrupted.

"No, he punched out one of the glass windows. I mean, the whole thing."

There were elongated windows just above the door knobs of each door on the third floor. They were hard, sturdy, and narrow. Looking at the doors, I wondered how his aim had been that good and where he had gotten such strength.

"How the hell did he do that?"

"Yeah, how did he do that?" Officer Travis repeated.

"Didn't you guys hear a word I said?" Ellway asked. "His father is Dominique White. The kid takes boxing lessons, and he is good."

"He didn't break his hand or anything?" I asked.

"Nah, Jay, and you know what? That's the same question I asked Willy when he told me the story. No broken hand. He just walked away huffin' and puffin'."

"Yeah, whatever. He's a punk just like the rest of these kids," Travis said, waiving his hand as if what Demetrius did was nothing.

"No, Travis, this kid fights older guys who are bigger and stronger. He ends up winning and embarrassing the other kid," Ellway said.

"Well, he can't beat me. I'll embarrass him," Travis responded.

"Of course he can't, Travis. He can't beat you, me, or Jay because we are big guys. We are probably the only three people in the building who aren't afraid of this kid. Ain't that right, Jay?"

"The boy needs his ass whipped. That will take care of everything," Travis blurted out, getting agitated.

"Travis, why do you always think someone needs their ass whipped?" I persisted.

"Because they do." Travis said, unconvincingly.

"Look, a kid like Demetrius White can take an ass whipping, get right back up, and start acting crazy again. You can't scare that kid—nothing can, and nothing ever will," Officer Ellway explained, staring into space.

"You know what, Ellway? You got much respect for this kid," Travis said.

"Hey, kiss my ass," Ellway shouted back after snapping out of his daze.

"The top cop doesn't kiss ass," Travis said.

"Yeah, you might be the top cop, but just remember, I'm the boss, top cop." Ellway and Travis often had arguments like this.

I did not even know if there was a boss among the school police at Parish Hill, but Ellway definitely had everyone thinking he was since he had been at the school the longest of all the officers. "Man, both of you are the silliest cops I've ever seen," I interjected.

"Hey, Jay, you don't do shit anyway except sit up there in your office and dress nice," Ellway joked as Travis and I laughed.

*   *   *

"We are truly in our last days, my brother. I do believe that we are truly in our last days." Those words Travis often said ran through my head as I watched Demetrius' latest altercation.

After hanging up the phone, Mr. Hazelton tried to calm Demetrius down on his own.

"Demetrius, don't run past me," Mr. Hazelton said as he stepped in front of the door so Demetrius could not leave the room.

"Get out of my way, man," Demetrius said in a frustrated, low voice.

"No. Demetrius, sit down. You are not leaving. I can't let you leave." Mr. Hazelton was not very aggressive, but he was trying to be firm. I respected him for that. He was an excellent teacher in a dysfunctional school, and he stood his ground. He never let the kids run over him during his lessons.

"Come on, man. Stop playin' wit me," Demetrius mumbled as he paced around in front of Mr. Hazelton and the doorway as the rest of the class watched.

"Sit down, Demetrius."

"Get the fuck out of my way!" Demetrius lunged toward Mr. Hazelton forcefully.

Mr. Hazelton remained in front of the door, blocking Demetrius' way out of the room. Demetrius bumped Mr. Hazelton as he tried to get by.

Although teachers are not supposed to touch students, Mr. Hazelton put his left arm out to stop Demetrius from leaving the room. Demetrius and Mr. Hazelton began to tussle.

"Don't fight with me, Demetrius," Mr. Hazelton was trying to hold Demetrius still with both arms and all of his might. Mr. Hazelton was a thin but athletic-looking Caucasian man who rode his bike to school every day.

Demetrius started breathing really hard. As he slammed Mr. Hazelton against the door, Mr. Hazelton, who had about three inches and fifteen pounds on Demetrius, was still able to walk.

"Demetrius, relax," Mr. Hazelton said calmly, maintaining his firm grip on Demetrius' shoulders. I knew Demetrius was about to reach his limit.

"Get the fuck off me!" he yelled out, cracking Mr. Hazelton right on the chin.

Mr. Hazelton's knees started to buckle. He would have fallen if he did not have Demetrius to hold on to while he gathered himself.

I had seen enough. I would have broken it up a lot earlier, but I was not part of the security team. I knew that physical interaction with the children, even in a situation like this, would be closely scrutinized by the principal. So, instead of intervening, I had stood by the stairs to wait for one of the hall monitors and the school police to come. School police had the authority to use force in situations like these, if necessary, but they rarely did. They were afraid Mrs. Matthews would reprimand them if they did.

By the time I made my mind up to risk getting in trouble by walking over to help break up the incident, the help Mr. Hazelton had called a few minutes earlier was on the way.

"Demetrius, come on man. Calm down," I said, trying to use my voice to calm him. He began to relax.

Mr. Hazelton let go of Demetrius, and he stood up straight – he was okay for the time being.

"Demetrius, why don't you go down to the counselors' suite and relax?" I asked as I hinted to Mr. Hazelton to hand Demetrius his jacket.

"Give me my fuckin' coat," he uttered. One of the students gave Demetrius his jacket, and he was off down the steps. He did not go to the counselors' suite. He left the building. I was hoping that he would not return because I did not know what he might return with.

"What the hell is going on? Are you okay, Mr. Hazelton?" Officer Caroll asked, out of breath from running the entire way. Officer Caroll was extremely overweight and had probably just come from handling another incident.

"I'm fine," Mr. Hazelton said, trying to catch his breath.

"Write everything down on a pink slip so we can get to the bottom of this," Officer Caroll said like it was a novel idea.

As Mr. Hazelton wrote on the pink slip, he kneeled down in the doorway and leaned back against the doorframe. "Do you need the nurse, Mr. Hazelton?" I asked.

He looked at me and shook his head, frowning his lips and raising one eyebrow, protecting his manhood. I nodded my head in acknowledgment and went down the stairs.

Mr. Hazelton was hurting, and he was hurting bad. He was not hurting as much physically as he was mentally and spiritually. A student, a 16-year-old special education student, had just drained all Mr. Hazelton had with one punch. His efforts, spunk, and enthusiasm were gone.

Mr. Hazelton was a good teacher. He should have been able to go into his classroom and teach his lessons in peace without having to worry about being assaulted in front of his class, but it was Parish Hill, and we all had to worry about these eruptions of violence.

As for Demetrius, nothing at all happened – standard procedure at Parish Hill. There was talk about consequences; it was rumored that as soon as Demetrius came back into Parish Hill, he would be arrested. Instead, after Mr. Hazelton turned in his report to the school police, the school police had a meeting. Then they let the administration know everything that had happened. As usual, as far as I or any other staff members knew, nothing happened.

Mr. Hazelton was one of the last teachers that anyone in the building would expect this to happen to, but there were two teachers who routinely ran into this kind of trouble.

Kushner and Leslie

"I say, what's goin' on dog? I'm in the smog, dog. You can't mess with me, cause I'm the boss hog."

"Shut the fuck up, Kushner," someone shouted out from the crowd of students in the hallway.

Mr. Kushner was an overweight white teacher at an all black school. This was the kind of response he normally received when he opened his mouth. Even if students did not verbalize it, they expressed it with their body language by walking away, making faces, or waving their hands at him in disapproval. Kushner had tried to obtain the kids' respect, but failed, and then gave up. This was one of his ways of giving up. He would mock the children by rapping and strolling up and down the hallway when the students switched classes.

Anyone could see that Kushner did not want to be at Parish Hill. He made it clear with his actions. The administration made it clear that they did not want him to be at Parish Hill either.

"What's going on, Kushner?" I said at the beginning of the day, walking toward my office, getting ready for the children to come upstairs for the day.

"Hey, Williams, did you ever do anything about the sexual harassment situation with Denise Jenkins?"

"That situation was never passed to me," I said. "I don't know anything about it."

"Yeah, well, I reported it," Kushner said in a soft voice, stepping closer to me.

"Who did you report it to?"

"I reported it to Ms. Gladstone, who should have reported it to Mrs. Matthews. I overheard one of the children talking about how Tyreak wants Denise to give him oral sex."

"How did you report it?"

"I wrote what I heard on a pink slip and gave it to her."

"To who?"

"I gave it to Gladstone and Matthews!"

"Kushner, they are not going to take that seriously."

"Why not?"

"Because it is secondhand."

"Well, they need to take it seriously. That's their fucking problem. They don't take anything seriously. And you know what? When these cameras come through here and put us all on the news, don't come crying to me. Matthews is trying to get rid of me. She's coming down hard on my ass—hard! But you know what? That's okay. I'll find work because I am qualified. I do my job, and I'm smart."

Kushner started to go off on a personal tirade. I was tired of standing in the hallway listening to him complain. This was not about sexual harassment. Kushner was trying to recruit people who felt the same way he did about Matthews and Gladstone, and he was failing.

"All right, Kushner. I'm going into my office. I'll talk to you later."

I went into my office and put my coat and bags away. Then I followed up on the Denise Jenkins issue. I wanted to make sure that, if true, something as serious as that was taken care of. I decided to do it in the privacy of my office, without the help of Kushner, because he had a big mouth and had already handled the situation the wrong way.

He should have talked to Denise first and written down what she had said instead of acting like one of the children and spreading rumors, but I was not going to tell Kushner that. He was stubborn and not willing to change. Further conversation with him would just have agitated me, and agitation was his specialty.

"I'll teach you how to lunch! My stomach's growling. I'm hungry, man. I'll teach you how to lunch!" I could hear that Kushner was at it again – rapping. He was in the hallway mimicking a rap song by 50 Cent, a popular rapper at the time. He was substituting the word "lunch" for the word "stunt," trying to get the lingering students to go upstairs to the cafeteria. This was the wrong way for Kushner to try to develop relationships; the students found it offensive.

"Hey, Kushner, you corny, dog," one of the students responded.

This just made Kushner add a non-rhythmic dance to his rhyme.

"I will teach you how to lunch! I'll teach you how to lunch! Yeah!" as he ended the performance, he swung his arm behind his lower back with his hand curved upward and started strutting, George Jefferson-style. Although Kushner occasionally received laughs from the students, he never received their respect.

How could they respect him? As soon as he was frustrated, he would start his rap routine. I had also heard about a few incidents where Kushner cursed at the students in his classroom. He was fed up and wanted out of Parish Hill, and the students could tell. They even tried to help him reach that goal.

"Hey, Mr. Williams," one of the students said, coming to my office and shaking my hand.

"What's going on?" I responded.

"We are taking this letter to Mrs. Matthews," he said.

The letter was written by some of Kushner's students who had gotten wind that Mrs. Matthews was trying to get rid of him. The letter explained that the students felt they were not learning anything in his class, needed more homework, and were tired of Kushner cursing and making racial remarks. He asked me to give it to Mrs. Matthews.

Parish Hill students seldom told on one another, they were solidly against "snitching," but when the teacher was wrong, they were all snitches. The teachers knew that, but they kept pushing the students' buttons.

I told him that I thought it would be best if the letter came from him or another student and that I was sure Mrs. Matthews would do what was best. Though, honestly, after hearing how the staff talked about her, I wasn't sure what she would do.

Teachers like Kushner kept playing with the students and treating everything like a joke, and that is exactly how they were treated in return.

He was not alone. Ms. Leslie was guilty of the same crime. The sad thing was that at the beginning of the year, she did have the kids' respect. When I came to the school in October, the students gravitated toward her, seeming to desire her approval.

Ms. Leslie yelled all the time. She never said anything in a calm voice. "One plus one is what, Devon?!"

"Two," Devon answered.

"Good! Okay! Glad to see that you have some common sense. Now, how come you can't follow simple rules and instructions? I said, put your pencils down after you are done with the test, not to doodle on the side of your desk and talk to your friends. Okay?!" I liked Ms. Leslie's message. I even liked her choice of words, but she really needed to lower her voice.

Her voice was annoying, but it was ultimately her own actions that led to her downfall at Parish Hill. She talked to the children about the right thing to do, but often did the wrong things to try to maintain their respect. Contradicting herself in front of her students gave them ammunition to misbehave.

*   *   *

I stood next to Willy as he sat in his hallway-watching chair. We were talking about the sporting events that happened over the weekend when I noticed something.

"Hey, Willy, why did the kids rip all the hallway decorations down?" I asked. "It's just the seventh grade floor. The sixth and eighth grade floors don't look like this."

"That's because Ms. Leslie has been showing her ass," Willy responded.

"What?"

"Yeah, she's been up here yelling at the kids like she is in charge of the floor, and the real person in charge of the floor is Mr. Kyle, the lead teacher. Kushner is following right behind her, too, and both of they asses are already in hot water."

"But she's been yelling at the children all year."

"Yeah, but Jay, she has really picked it up in the last month or so, and the kids are getting tired of all her bullshit sarcasm, yelling, and screaming. So, they ripped down the decorations that her and Kushner put up."

"They ripped everything down, huh? They were pretty bad, but at least they gave the hallway some life."

"Yeah, but that ain't all they did, Jay," Willy said leaning in as if he had something very important to tell me.

Willy pulled a napkin out of his pocket to wipe the beads of sweat off his bald head. He took a deep breath and slowly opened his eyes. Then he jumped out of his seat. "Hey kids, I'm tired of telling y'all. I am really tired of telling y'all the same thing over and over again. Get back in the classroom. Sharice, Chris, Jalen, Sandra—all y'all about to get a phone call to your house," Willy said. He sat back down and picked up where he left off.

"What else man, what else happened?" I prodded.

"Leslie was letting the kids have sex in there."

"Yo! What did you just say?" I asked in disbelief.

"Yeah, you heard me!"

"That's ridiculous."

"Nah, seriously, Jay, that's real. Now she is trying to put an end to it. The only thing is, the students are giving her hell about it. Could you imagine her one day coming in school and saying, 'Okay y'all, that's enough. No more fuckin' in my room.' These kids would laugh their ass off and start sayin' crazy things to her like, 'Hey Leslie, how come you lettin' kids have sex in your room?'"

"These kids wouldn't do that."

"Jay, I have been working here for seven years. Not only would they say it, but they'd say it while Mrs. Matthews or Ms. Gladstone walked by."

"If Ms. Leslie has been letting the kids do this, then she deserves whatever comes her way. This is going to end up hurtin' her bad. She is tryin' to be cool with the students."

"But Jay, in all reality, she is just here for a paycheck. She doesn't really care about these kids because if she did, she wouldn't be letting them do all the things they do in her room. It's just a matter of time before all this catches up to her."

"All right Willy, I'll talk to you later. I have to go make some phone calls," I said, sighing and walking to my office at the other end of the hallway.

"Okay, Jay. I'll talk to you later."

Tested

Back in my office, I tried to digest the news Willy had just told me.

I sat down at my desk and started thinking about how things were for me when I first came to Parish Hill.

"Hey, hey, counselor boy." That was how many of the students addressed me during my first few weeks at Parish Hill. Because I was young, I was tested in all types of ways. Twenty-five years old – that was only eight years older than the oldest seventh grader.

And my office was right in the middle of the action, on the worst floor in the school – the third floor, full of seventh graders who did not respond well to authority.

"What? Ha, ha, ha!" one student said on my first day, raising his hand as if he were going to hit me. I didn't flinch. I didn't even make a facial expression. I just looked down at the student like he was crazy.

When he saw that I was not scared, he quickly walked away and said, "Oh yeah, that's what I thought." This was all that many of the kids had. They did not come to school to get an education. They came to school to cause mischief and seek acceptance from their peers. These children would do anything to get their friends' respect, even if it meant "chumping," or trying to scare a teacher.

The girls also engaged in chumping, but they were mischievous in an entirely different way – a way that any decent man would detest. My first warning about this kind of behavior came from Mrs. Matthews.

I was often skeptical of Mrs. Matthews' advice because I disagreed with her decisions about the students, but the advice she gave me on my first day at Parish Hill could not have been more accurate.

*   *   *

"Mr. Williams, this is your first day at Parish Hill. Have you ever worked at an inner city school before?

"Yes I have, but not for a whole year."

"Well, I am going to tell you that these girls are going to think of you as a friend," she said, lowering her glasses to the tip of her nose.

I just sat there and tilted my head to the side inquisitively.

"You have to be careful because you are an attractive young man, and you aren't much older than them. They are going to really try and take advantage of the fact that you are a counselor and come to your office when they should be in class."

*   *   *

For my first month at Parish Hill, it seemed like Mrs. Matthews had been in my shoes before. The female students at Parish Hill would knock on my door asking to talk about some issues they had. I would let them in if it sounded like they had something that was really a concern.

"Hey, Mr. Williams, I need to talk to you."

"About what? What's wrong?"

"The boys keep messin' with me. Here's my pass."

If the students had a pass to see me, it was usually because their teacher had sent them for misbehaving. I was new to the game. I didn't know that the students sometimes wrote fake passes and that staff could call to check. After this charade, I started following that procedure

"Can I come in?" she asked innocently.

"Yes, come in." As I turned my back to the door, three other girls came into the office.

"Hold on, what are you guys doing? You can't just come in here. Where are your passes?" I asked, confused but calm.

"We don't have passes," one of the girls said.

"Well look, ladies, you know you need to—" before I could finish I was cut off with a barrage of questions.

"Is this your computer?"

"Can I use the phone?"

"Mr. Williams, can I open a window?"

They thought quickly and talked fast.

"You guys are really trying to make yourselves at home aren't you?"

As this was going on, I had taken a seat at my desk. My eyes were off the girl who had asked for help because I was focused on the other three girls running around my office.

"Look, you young ladies have to go. I have to help Tiffany. She is the only one out of all of you that has a pass."

When I turned my head back to Tiffany, she had taken her school uniform shirt off, unveiling a see-through shirt and the bra underneath.

"Yeah, that's right, Mr. Williams is tryin' to help me," she said as she tried to sit on my lap and throw her arms around my neck.

I quickly pushed her off, upset. I wanted all of them out of my office because their behavior was completely inappropriate.

"It is time for you guys to leave," I said, standing up.

"Come on, Williams," one of them said as she slowly walked to the door.

"No. There is no 'come on.' You get out."

Not responding well to authority, two of the young ladies stopped short of the door. I guided them out the doorway and shut the door.

Teachers were tested like this, and in other ways, on a daily basis. Cursing, fighting – all of this occurred in the hallways of Parish Hill right in front of our eyes. How we responded told the children whether we cared about their well-being. When I had to deal with two students fighting, I responded by breaking up the fight. It hurt me to see children fighting like that, and they fought hard, too.

The first fight I broke up happened in a classroom.

"Oh, Lord! Oh, my God!" The teacher yelled, running from the room. She was running down the hallway like the place was on fire. "They're fighting, and there's nothing I can do! I need help," she shouted.

I heard the desks sliding across the floor. I went into the classroom and found about fifty kids gathered around two girls. The students had come from other classes and floors. I was telling the girls to stop, but they did not hear me. When I reached the two girls, I grabbed one of them with my right hand, one of them with my left hand, and pulled them apart.

"What's the matter with y'all?" I asked. "Cut it out."

Everyone gasped. I thought they were amazed at my strength, but that was not the case: Apparently, they were not used to seeing a teacher or counselor stop a fight. Not many, if any, of the teachers would break up a fight because it was against the rules, but I could not stand watching two little girls fight like that.

"Come on, let's go." The students watched me escort the girls down to the second floor so the girls could talk to Ms. Gladstone.

When I brought them into vice principal Gladstone's office, she gave me a funny look. It was different from the look the students had given me. The students had looked surprised that I cared enough to break up the fight, but Ms. Gladstone's facial expression said, "This guy is crazy! What is he doing? He can't bring these kids in here like that. Besides, what does he want me to do with them?"

"Ms. Gladstone, these two young women were fighting upstairs. Maybe you could help them talk about their problems and give them the punishment they deserve," I said, backing out. "I have a parent coming in to talk about high school selection."

The way I handled these incidents showed the students and teachers that I cared and that I was not afraid, which built the students' respect for me.

Kushner's Fall

"Yeah, go to class. Get the hell out of the hallway before I get my main man Williams to dunk on you. What's up, Jay?" Kushner called out.

He was still excited about the recent annual student-staff game. Four staff members and I had beaten the student team. That had never happened at Parish Hill, and it earned us the students' respect – well, everyone except Kushner, but that was his fault.

"Hey, what's up Kushner?" I answered mildly, entering my office.

He hadn't learned anything after that game. He was still acting like one of the kids. He was still letting the whole world know he was frustrated, by wearing his feelings on his sleeve. After the game, everything Kushner said in retaliation to a child acting out referenced the staff victory on the court. This went on for about a month until his classroom door window was smashed, along with a few other teachers.

Willy didn't even know who broke the windows, and he knew everything. I saw it as a strategic move by the students. They had smashed Kushner's window because they were tired of his sarcasm and mockery. It stayed that way for a long time, so as students walked by Kushner's room, they threw small objects at him through the space, shouting, "Fuck you, Kushner!" and running.

A Nightmare for Ms. Leslie

Things had only gotten worse for Ms. Leslie after she tried to bargain for the students' respect by letting them have sex in her classroom.

"Oooh, oooh, I'm tellin'. You guys are not supposed to be doin' that in the hallway." No, this was not the voice of a student; it was Ms. Leslie sounding like one of them. She also looked like one of the students, dressed in a Donovan McNabb Mitchel & Ness jersey, baggy jeans, and a pair of Timberland boots. She had just seen two students kissing in the hallway.

They paid her no mind and continued with what they were doing. Angry that her authority was being ignored, Ms. Leslie said, "Okay, you know what? Since y'all won't stop, I'm calling Bianca's father." When Bianca heard this, she stopped for a moment and then resumed kissing her boyfriend, Terrance. They thought Ms. Leslie was just joking, as she often did, but this time she was serious. Ms. Leslie called Mr. Maddox, and he came immediately. He didn't get there fast enough to catch Bianca and Terrance kissing, but he did catch Bianca running around, chasing other students, and hanging out the hallway window. She ignored Willy when he told her to stop, and her father witnessed the whole thing.

"Bianca, get over here!" Mr. Maddox shouted down the hallway as Bianca fled. "Now that's another strike," her father said to himself with disgust. Strike one was that he saw her disrespect Willy who was a close friend of his.

But she did not get away. She ran right into her father when he walked down the nearest staircase and cornered her on the second floor.

"What is wrong with you, Bianca?" he asked.

"Uh—uh—" shocked, she couldn't come up with anything.

"Come on, we're going back upstairs to speak to Ms. Leslie."

Leslie was already at the top of the stairs waiting for them to come up to the third floor. "Bianca, Bianca," Ms. Leslie said, shaking her head back and forth, hand on her hip. An audience of students had formed in the hallway, so I guess Ms. Leslie felt it was necessary to perform, which was a big mistake.

"Bianca, you know you was wrong up here kissin' Terrance like that." All of a sudden the hallway got extremely quiet. It was obvious the students knew something Ms. Leslie did not.

Mr. Maddox's eyes were as wide as saucers. "You were kissing in the hallway?" he asked, souring his face as if he had a bad taste in his mouth.

He squinted at Bianca for about ten seconds. She stared back with a blank expression.

All of a sudden, out of nowhere, "Crrrack!" Mr. Maddox smacked Bianca in the mouth. Not only did she cry, she bled.

She took off running, and he calmly walked down the stairs and out the building. This left Ms. Leslie in the hallway with the audience, which consisted of Terrance, his crew, and a bunch of followers who were sick and tired of Ms. Leslie. At this point, Ms. Leslie's teaching career was forever altered.

"Bitch, why the fuck you do that?" Terrance erupted, breaking the silence.

"Who you callin' a bitch?" Ms. Leslie shouted back.

"You!" Terrance answered with conviction.

"Hey, Leslie, that was fucked up, man," another member of the crowd blurted out.

"Yeah, Leslie, damn. Why you have to call her father? You always tryin' to start some shit. You knew that man was gonna come up here and do what he did. You a snitch," one of Terrance's crew said with a look of disgust.

Ms. Leslie was standing outside her classroom with twenty students gathered around her cursing at, interrogating, and testing her.

"All right, everyone, get back to class," she said with a blank look on her face. She was confused. She was not used to being disrespected like that, and it scared her. She knew she had handled the situation the wrong way, not only because Bianca had gotten smacked in the mouth, but because Ms. Leslie had contradicted herself. Terrance and Bianca were two of the students who were rumored to have permission to have sex in her classroom. Not only had she made a call for a parent, she had made a call for trouble.

"Come on y'all, get back to class. Let's go," she said clapping her hands and walking toward the crowd of students who were already starting to disperse – all except for Terrance and his group of four. He stood there staring Ms. Leslie down until she went back into her classroom.

Ms. Leslie walked into her classroom backwards, keeping her eyes on Terrance as she closed the door slowly. She knew that he was the most respected boy in the seventh grade. He might have been feared more than respected. He had a reputation for carrying large amounts of money in his pockets; money he got from dealing drugs. Terrance's crew would do whatever he told them to do.

The next day Ms. Leslie went off school grounds to get lunch. When she came back, her room was completely trashed. She immediately knew who was responsible. Terrance and his crew had ransacked the classroom. Desks were overturned, computers were knocked over, and pictures and chairs had been thrown out the window.

This hurt Ms. Leslie. She didn't cry, but her ego was deeply bruised. It was the first time in her four years working at Parish Hill that something even close to this magnitude had happened to her. Ms. Leslie rounded up a few kids who were still loyal to her to help her get her room back in order.

The next time Terrance had Ms. Leslie's class, things erupted.

While teaching, she started using all types of unnecessary, off-topic examples.

"Like for example, if someone destroys your room and throws stuff out the window, then what should happen to that person? Can anyone tell me? Terrance? Terrance! Why don't you tell me, Terrance?"

She was helping someone else with their reading and kept referring to Terrance and using his name in an example. Terrance was sitting on the other side of the classroom ignoring her and talking to a friend sitting next to him.

Willy filled me in on the details on what happened to Leslie during our next hallway encounter.

"Yo, what's goin' on, Jay?"

"What's happenin', Will?"

"Y'all Lakers was strugglin' against Houston, that's what. How much money did y'all pay the refs to win in overtime the way y'all did? Y'all should have lost that game, man."

"Look, we pulled the game out. That's all that matters."

"It must be nice to sit around and do nothing except talk about basketball all day. Some of us actually have to work," Kushner said sarcastically as he stood in the doorway of his classroom, watching Willy and me. It was the last period of the day, and we were unwinding in front of my office. Willy was standing, pacing back and forth, and I was sitting on a desk.

"Mind your business," Willy snapped.

"Yeah, Kushner, mind your business and root for your Sixers. Oh, my fault. They didn't even make the playoffs," I said, chuckling.

"Hey Williams, fuck you," Kushner whispered before going back into the classroom and closing the door.

Willy was cracking up. "Kushner is heated."

"Where is his sidekick?" I asked.

"You didn't hear about Leslie?"

"I heard a little bit. I know that Terrance and his boys ransacked her room."

"That's not why she's out, Jay After that incident, she told the cops that Terrance pushed her."

"What?"

"Yeah, Officer Cleveland came up here and was questioning her, Terrance, and about five other boys who were trying to get this other boy, David, who she was hiding in her room.

"They were at the door yelling at David, who was standing behind Ms. Leslie. They were telling him that they were going to fuck him up, and David was telling them that they weren't going to do shit, and Leslie was actually backing him up, standing in front of him like she was his body guard. Talkin' about, 'Yeah, y'all ain't gonna do shit.' I mean she was cursing and everything. All that did was make the boys angry. The boys ran through Leslie, knocked her over, and started whipping David's ass. They were beating him up because he had stolen Tyreak's cell phone and had been getting on their nerves all year."

"Wait. They knocked her over?"

"Exactly, Jay, they knocked her over. Not Terrance, but Tyreak and the rest of them knocked her over. Terrance was the last person to go in the room, so he couldn't have knocked her over. Leslie told Cleveland that Terrance did it."

"If Terrance didn't knock her over, then why would she say he—" in the middle of my sentence, I realized that she was trying to get Terrance in trouble because she suspected that he trashed her room.

After thinking about everything, I looked back at Willy, and he was looking at me with a grin. "That's why she hasn't been back in the building, Jay She pressed charges on Terrance, and she isn't coming back for the rest of the year. She put in for a stress leave. I saw her at the bar and told her she was doing the right thing."

"She what? That's crazy! We're short-staffed as it is. They got me covering two classes a day."

"I heard when Officer Cleveland was questioning her," Willy continued, "she was reaching for anything. She told him the real story first. Cleveland told her he couldn't do anything because all Terrance had done was talk trash. Then he asked her, 'Well, did he threaten you or assault you?' And she said, 'Oh yeah, yeah, he pushed me and said he was going to kill me.' Now, Jay, I heard he said he was going to kill her, but she had threatened to cut him with a knife first."

"A knife?"

"Yeah, I think she was talking about that knife she keeps in her purse."

"How do you know about that?"

"Jay, I know everything."

"You know too much.

"That's my job," he said, chuckling.

Like Kushner, Leslie's actions finally caught up to her. Instead of being professional and responsible adults, they had joined the children.

Marlow

"CDs, DVDs! CDs, DVDs!" It sounded like I was on the subway or walking down South Street by a guy trying to sell some bootleg merchandise, but I wasn't. I was in my office and listening to what could have been a student about to get in a lot of trouble or a trespasser trying to make an extra dollar, but it wasn't. It was the lead teacher of the sixth grade, the head coach of the eighth grade boys' basketball team, Mr. Marlow.

Marlow might as well have been a trespasser trying to make a few dollars, because money was all he cared about, and he didn't care what he did to make it. When I first came to Parish Hill, I thought he was a sincere teacher who did his job. I was wrong; I consistently saw him take shortcuts and bring the streets into the school.

"CDs, DVDs! CDs, DVDs! Whatever you need, I got it. Get your CDs and DVDs! Yo, Williams, I got that new Tupac! What you need?"

"No, I'm okay," I said, as if it was no big deal that he was corrupting the students' minds, boosting within the school. I wanted to erupt, but I remained calm because I was just a substitute. He had been doing things like this for eight years, carefully avoiding the second floor because that's where the administration was.

"Come on, Williams," he said as he waved his hand with a smile on his face, knowing I already had a tight grip on my money. "I'll talk to you later." He knew I would not buy one of his CDs or DVDs because I couldn't stand what they represented. This was an institution for learning, a place where students were supposed to come and expand their minds, mature mentally, and grow academically. How could the kids feel compelled to accomplish those things when they saw the lead teacher of the sixth grade selling bootleg products?

Marlow did not come to school to teach, he came to make money. And in the process of making money, he showed the children how to be slick and get over in life.

He didn't stop with the CDs and DVDs. He sold candy, glowing heart necklaces, and pens. He also sold Mitchell and Ness Throw Back Jerseys for $150 to kids who were supposed to wear uniforms to school.

The only thing Marlow was good for was suspending people. I knew of five people in the building who had that authority: Mrs. Matthews, Ms. Gladstone, the lead teacher of the seventh grade, the lead teacher of the eighth grade, and Marlow.

"You can't come to school dressed in a suit all the time. You have to dress like these kids do every once in a while," Marlow said one day. "Come in this motherfucker wearing a suit every day, and these kids are gonna think you're a joke."

"Yeah, but these kids have a dress code to follow, Marlow. They have to abide by the rules of the school," Travis responded.

"Yeah, but you can't—" Marlow sucked his teeth and started pacing back and forth, not finishing his sentence, as usual. Marlow often mumbled and spoke unclearly when he said something questionable. "Look, man, you just can't wear a suit every day," Marlow finished, frustrated that Travis didn't agree with his gibberish. He shook his head while he spoke, acting like Travis didn't know what he was talking about.

"Y'all got to realize," Marlow said as he picked his teeth. "All these kids understand is money. Michael Jordan wouldn't be Michael Jordan if it wasn't for the shoes," Marlow said, spouting more garbage.

"What?" I replied.

"He wouldn't be Michael Jordan if it wasn't for the shoes. Look at how many people in the hood buy Jordans. That man wouldn't be who he is today if it wasn't for the shoes."

"Are you serious, Marlow?" Officer Travis asked. "That man got where he is because of perseverance and hard work, my brother! If it wasn't for Michael Jordan, the shoes wouldn't be what they are. There have been plenty of athletes who have come out with a shoe that has been unsuccessful because they were unsuccessful. Hard work, time, and effort made Mike, and after that, Mike made the shoes." The whole time Travis was talking, Marlow was pacing back and forth, shaking his head.

"Hey, Marlow, you're messed up," I told him, leaning forward and looking him in the eye. "You just don't get it, do you? You think that the only thing the kids understand is money. Well, fine, then it is your job to teach them otherwise, not to sit back and abuse their weaknesses and sell your products."

"Abuse their weaknesses? Abuse their weaknesses? Williams, what are you talking about?" He looked at me as if I was speaking a foreign language.

At this point, I was furious. I was tired of talking. Marlow made me feel like I was talking to a child who just could not fit common sense into his thought pattern. I took a step towards him, and this time it wasn't to tell him how misguided his thinking was.

"Williams, relax, man," Travis said, holding me back and laughing at the same time. He had been at this point with Marlow before, and I had held him back.

"You're a crooked bastard. Your thought pattern, attitude – your whole persona is going to get you in a lot of trouble one day, if it hasn't already," I told him, pointing my finger at him.

Marlow just walked away. He went downstairs to his floor, where the kids used to look up to him until they found out that all he was good for was selling things and suspending people.

Marlow did have the respect of a few of the parents, though. He would call home and talk to them about their children if they were acting up or being disruptive. I applauded Marlow on that because communication with the parents was important and often overlooked, and the students usually benefited when it occurred.

But there was one parent who Marlow did not have a close bond with.

"Get in your reading groups," Marlow said to the class. They quickly got into their groups as he had ordered, but for some reason, he was still not happy. "I said get in your reading groups. Your reading groups. Your reading groups!" He said with authority as he walked closer and closer to a girl who was sitting in the wrong group. "What's the matter with you? Hey! Are you hard of hearing? I said get in your reading groups!"

The student did not acknowledge Marlow. I don't think she even knew Marlow was talking to her since he hadn't said her name.

By now, he was extremely irritated. He wasn't getting the respect he desired and felt he deserved. After all, he was the lead teacher of the sixth grade.

Marlow started poking the girl on the shoulder as he shouted, "Reading groups, reading groups, reading groups!"

"Don't poke me on my shoulder, motherfucker!" the young lady snapped.

"You're suspended," Marlow responded.

"Fine. I don't care, but wait 'til I get home and tell my mother that you were poking me on my shoulder like you had no sense."

"That is exactly why you should have moved when I told you to. Then maybe you wouldn't have been poked on the shoulder."

"Well, you shouldn't have put your hands on me." The girl got up, got her things from her locker, and left the building.

Thinking she had received the maximum penalty – a three-day suspension – the girl did not come to school the next day. But her mother did. I was walking around the corner near the main office when I bumped into Officer Caroll.

"Williams, I've been looking for you. When you get around this corner, let me know what you see," she said, ecstatic.

I turned the corner and saw Marlow, Officer Travis, a fat man, and a woman even larger than the man. The woman had her finger right between Marlow's eyes, and her face wasn't far behind it, yelling harsh words.

I looked to my right, and I saw Officer Caroll laughing hysterically. She was so glad to see someone putting Marlow in his place that she didn't know what to do with herself. I thought back to an incident that explained exactly why she was getting so much pleasure out of this whole ordeal: I remembered sitting in the school police office waiting for Officer Travis to come in with one of the students I had been helping get on the right track. The student had relapsed and had been involved in an incident, and I wanted to know what had happened. While I was sitting in the office by myself, Marlow came in with two girls.

"What's up, Williams?" Marlow asked as if we were on good terms.

"What's up Marlow?" I played along.

He sucked his teeth and replied, "Nothing. I'm about to finish getting my hair braided so I can look fly on this trip." I hadn't noticed when he walked in, but his hair was half braided and half afro.

Not only was Marlow having issues with his hair, he was over 30 and had on a 76ers throwback jersey, jeans, and Timberlands. I was beginning to think that this was the Parish Hill teacher uniform. For the "lead teacher of the sixth grade academy," which is how Marlow often referred to himself, this was poor representation.

The whole scene was absurd. Marlow was sitting down, one girl behind him doing his hair and the other girl sitting to his right. There were two desks in the police office, and I was sitting at the one closest to the door, my mouth hanging open.

"Yo, you have to put some grease in there," Marlow said to the young lady with her hands in his hair.

"All right, Marlow, damn," the girl said back.

She wasn't wearing a school uniform, so I figured she was one of Marlow's female companions. But the longer I waited for Travis, the more I got the sense that these girls were students. When Officer Caroll exploded into the room, I was sure of it. "What is this? A hair convention?" Officer Caroll asked.

"Yeah," Marlow said in a sly voice.

"Get these kids out of here!"

"Get these kids out of here, or you'll do what?" Marlow snapped back at her.

"Get these kids out of here, or I will go upstairs and tell Matthews that you're running a salon in my office!" Caroll screamed.

"Well, go ahead and tell Matthews then," Marlow said, waving his hand.

"I will!" Caroll responded, walking out.

"Yeah, you do that," Marlow squeezed in, battling for the last word.

"Get the fuck out of my office!" Caroll shouted over her shoulder as she stormed upstairs to see principal Matthews.

Five minutes later, Officer Ellway came into the office and told Marlow that Mrs. Matthews wanted to see him in the hallway. Marlow sucked his teeth and grinned, looking back and forth at Ellway and me. Tilting his head down, he walked into the hall with the girls not far behind.

"What was he thinking?" I asked.

"What happened, Jay?" Ellway wanted to know.

"I'm sittin' in here waiting for Travis, and Marlow comes in here with these two students; and one of them was doing his hair."

"What? Marlow knows better than that. Oh, shit—" something had jolted Ellway's memory. "That's what Caroll was saying. Only thing I really understood her say was 'girls' and 'Marlow,' and the next thing I know, Matthews was one step behind me on her way down here."

Ellway peeked his head out the door. "Jay, come here," he chuckled softly. I looked out the door and saw Mrs. Matthews giving a lecture. I have to admit it was rather funny; Marlow's hair was half done, and he was dressed like a teenager getting ready to go to a party.

As I turned my thoughts back to the present and took my eyes off Carroll, I saw Marlow put his hands in the air like he was being held up at gunpoint. As I got closer, I heard the robust woman say in a very calm but firm tone, "If you put your hands on my daughter again, you will not be teaching here anymore. You will not be breathing, either. As a matter of fact, they're gonna find your ass somewhere stinkin'."

"Well, well, well, I guess we are done talkin' then," Marlow said and proceeded through the doors to the opposite end of the hallway.

"Yeah, you better walk away, you little coward," the woman said.

Marlow was pretty solemn for the next two days. He was not his usual self. There was no mumbling, grinning, or sucking of teeth coming from Marlow's direction after that. He was embarrassed and scared. He was not going from floor to floor selling his goods and talking out the side of his mouth. That didn't last long, though, because after those two days of being mute, I heard Marlow coming around the corner chanting, "Twizzlers, one dollar, and Skittles, fifty cent. Get 'em while they're hot."

Ellway Joins the 'Oh No!'s

Marlow was a bad teacher; his behavior had a negative effect on the children. That was easy to tell on the surface. Ellway's negative behavior, on the other hand, took time for me to recognize. When he, someone I thought was walking the straight and narrow, became unstable, I started to feel hopeless for the school as a whole.

Ellway was having a hard time in his personal life. One time he sat in my office and cried, telling me how his wife was cheating on him and he had to kick the door down to enter his own house, where she showered him with profanity and called law enforcement to have him removed.

After he told me that story, he was never quite the same. He sat in his office a lot more and had a very detached attitude, doing things that I never thought he would.

On one occasion, Ellway and I caught a student trying to break into my office with a master key. He made the student empty his pockets, confiscated the key, and then scolded the student before returning his belongings. I mentioned how good it was that he had located the key and could turn it in to Ms. Gladstone. He just looked at me and put the key in his pocket. He never made the report to Gladstone or did the paper work. He kept the key for himself. He was looking at me relying on the unwritten rule that I wouldn't tell anyone; that I would not snitch. I just looked back at him and shook my head. Not only was he jeopardizing his job, he was jeopardizing mine as well.

On another occasion, I overheard a child outside my office talking about how he had dropped a 'seed of weed' on the ground and Ellway had picked it up, handed it to him, and told him to be careful. The kid said Ellway kept walking and didn't even turn around.

Two weeks later, while Willy and I were having one of our discussions, he told me that Ellway had been suspended. Ellway's wife called the school and told Matthews that he had been taking drugs off the kids and bringing them home. The school put him on suspension while they investigated the matter. With a call like that coming in from outside the school, they couldn't take any chances – they had to get Ellway out of the school until they found answers.

Matthews and Gladstone were probably happy that Ellway was out of the building because the rumor had started making its way to the students. But I know for sure that there was one person that was not pleased that he was gone, and that was Officer Travis.

Lakara

The noise got louder and louder as I walked toward the doors that led to the 25th street-side of the school. I opened the doors and saw nothing but chaos. The block to my right was filled with people yelling, cursing, screaming, and crying. Grunts and obscenities filled the air. There were more than 30 children and people from the neighborhood out in the street fighting. At least another 70 people were standing around watching. Some people were standing on top of each other; others were on top of cars, jumping up and down. As I walked away from the school, I could hear roofs of cars caving in and windows and windshields shattering.

I glanced back at the scene and saw Officer Travis running into the crowd, trying to break up the massive fight. Officer Cleveland and his officers ran past me, toward the mob. Not far behind them were at least seven police cars and a wagon, all headed for the ruckus.

I was shocked at the scale of the fight and wondered if someone was going to lose their life. It reminded me of a brawl I had witnessed at the civic center years before. That fight had also involved a lot of people, but there was one disturbing difference. The fight at the civic center was between boys during a high school basketball game; this fight involved people of all ages.

It had started as a quarrel between two seventh grade girls, ages 13 and 15 – Lakara Johnson and Krystal Sanders. To my knowledge, Krystal attacked Lakara. That was the wrong thing to do because she was dealing with Lakara.

The next day, Travis banged on my office door. "Good brother, open up!" he yelled.

"Yo, what's up, man? How are you? You okay?" I asked, concerned that something may have happened to him during the mayhem.

"Yeah, I'm fine."

"What happened to you yesterday? I saw you running into that crowd. How did that go?"

"Lakara is crazy. That girl has a loud mouth and all she does is fight and cause trouble."

*   *   *

It was true – she caused a lot of problems at the school. I had been told that even her first day at Parish Hill was problematic because she was on house arrest. She came to school with a Lowjack on her right ankle and her probation officer on her left arm to make sure that she went to class.

Lakara pretty much ran the whole school, and she was in the seventh grade. There may have been two or three boys who did not fear her, but they were very tough.

Before Ellway's leave of absence, Lakara had been fighting in the third floor hallway a few lockers down from my office. I was sitting at my desk just after lunch. Children were getting ready to go to their classes, and all I heard was, "Pussy, get the fuck away from my girl." It sounded like something a boy would say, but Lakara had said it while sticking up for one of her flunkies, protecting her from some boy.

After she yelled at him, she ran up, punched him in the back of the head, jumped on his back, and started choking him and biting his shoulder at the same time.

The only person willing to break up a fight involving Lakara came running around the corner. It was Mr. Kyle, the lead teacher of the seventh grade. He was wearing a grey double-breasted suit with a black mock neck shirt underneath and a pair of black Cole Hans.

"Lakara, get off Rasheed, girl," he yelled while separating the two, but this did not stop Lakara. She went right back at Rasheed fast, hard, and strong with punches and kicks. The only problem was Mr. Kyle was still between them, and he was on one leg pressed up against the lockers. If his back hadn't been against the lockers, he would have fallen over.

"Somebody get Lakara!" he shouted as he stood in front of Lakara's target, Rasheed, who was fighting back, but barely.

Soon, Ellway ran up the steps and put Lakara in hand cuffs so he could carry her down to his office. "Come on, babygirl, you gotta come with me."

"I didn't do shit, Ellway. Rasheed was messin' with my girl Caren, and I don't play that shit. Take these fucking cuffs off me!"

"Lakara, calm down. You know you're out of order. Just be quiet and enjoy the walk."

That was Lakara's M.O. She always called staff by their last name without saying mister or miss, and whenever trouble occurred and she was involved, she was always the victim.

*   *   *

"So what happened yesterday, Travis?"

"Dog, before I could even get outside to my post, Lakara and Krystal were out in the middle of the street fighting. I was the only Parish Hill officer out there; Ellway's not here, fat-ass Caroll and mule-brain Farell were nowhere to be found."

"Damn, man! They hung you out to dry."

"Right! I mean, damn, can a brother get some help? So, I'm running out to them through the crowd. Yo, Williams, it was so many people out there. It had to be at least 300 or so because not only were kids from Parish Hill watching, but kids from Arsen High were there, too!"

"Wow," I responded.

"Yeah, but do you know what is really disturbing?"

"What?" I asked.

"The parents," Travis responded.

"Parents?"

"I can see children fighting one another and even their friends helping out. But grown folks—parents and shit—were out there joining in, punching and stomping kids and getting punched and stomped by kids. It was crazy."

"Man, you're just tryin' to be funny. I didn't see parents out there when I was on the way to the train," I said, waving my hand.

"B-B-B-Brother, not hardly," Travis stuttered into serious mode to let me know he was not playing around.

"You know our friend was out there," he said.

"Who?"

"Shaena."

"Why was she out there? I know she's not friends with Lakara, and I don't think she's friends with Krystal."

"She's not friends with either one of them, but someone said something she didn't like, and she just jumped in it. You know how that girl is, and she is strong as shit, and her mom knocked Ellway down on the ground like he was a little toddler when you first got here. She had him on the floor, shuffling around, calling for backup like a bitch," Travis laughed.

"Yo, man, you ain't right," I laughed along with him.

"Yeah, but fat-ass Shaena was out there with two grown women on her arms, spinning them around like she was a windmill. I got to her and held her down on the ground, but she was tryin' to fight with me. But I kept her down because by then the police officers showed up, and they were taking people away."

"Did they get Lakara?"

"No, I think Cleveland broke her and the other girls up and sent them in separate directions. Cleveland doesn't like seeing black kids go to jail, but the other cops were grabbing anyone they could get their hands on and chuckin' them in the back of the wagon, handcuffed and head first. Man, it was crazy how they were tossing them in there. I had to write so many reports, I didn't get home until six o'clock, and I live right across the street!"

Just then, Lakara peeked through the glass of my office door. "Yo, let me in, y'all."

I reached over and opened the door.

"Yo, what's up, Williams? What's up Travis?" Lakara stormed into the room, and two girls followed behind her. She sat on the opposite side of the table facing Travis.

"You guys should be in jail," Travis blurted out with a grin, glad that Lakara and her friends were in school and safe.

"Travis, look, we didn't have nothin' to do with it," Lakara said, speaking for everybody. "We were mindin' our own business tryin' to get home, and that bitch started talking shit."

"So she just started talking shit, huh? Is that why you guys had friends, family, and relatives out there helping you? Come on, Lakara, y'all knew you were going to fight. Don't even try to play me like that," Travis said.

"That's because she was talking shit all day."

"I heard that Krystal was standing up to you because you were talking shit to her in school that morning out in the hallway. Tell me that ain't true," Travis said.

"Look, that bitch got a lot of mouth," Lakara said, ignoring the fact that Travis knew what he was talking about. "She was talkin' 'bout she was gonna call up her sister and her mom if I didn't shut up."

"And I know you didn't shut up," Travis added. I chuckled shortly, acknowledging Travis from my desk as I kept working, never looking up or giving Lakara any attention, just focusing on my work.

I could feel her staring at me before she resumed. "Anyway, I called up my peeps so I didn't get jumped, and we were still outnumbered. She had way more people than we did."

"Yep," one of Lakara's crew agreed.

"But we held it down, though. We had a few of my cousins and little Stephanie."

"Stephanie?" I asked, turning around in my chair in a state of shock.

"Yeah, Williams, Stephanie was out there scrappin' hard. All these people in the school with all that mouth that claim to be down with me, this, that, and the third, and the only person backing up her words was little Stephanie."

I had thought of Stephanie as a good girl who stayed out of trouble. I was wrong. "Did she get hurt?"

"Nope, but she knocked a few people upside their heads. Damn!" Lakara started to slap hands and laugh with her girls.

I turned back around, irritated and angry with the news and the fact that Lakara was treating the whole thing as a joke.

"See, that's the problem. Y'all take everything as a joke. Now, if someone got killed yesterday, you wouldn't be over there joking about it, or would you?" Travis said inquisitively.

"What happened yesterday was no joke, and we don't think it was. Don't get it twisted," Lakara said.

"It was on the news," Travis replied, looking annoyed.

"What was on the news?" one of Lakara's girls asked, leaning forward.

"The fight. Well, not the actual fight, but they showed the intersection where the fight was. Y'all are giving our people a bad name," Travis said softly as he put his head down, looking drained.

"Travis, don't even go there, all right. What about Matthews and this fuckin' school? This school fuckin' sucks. She ain't makin' it no better. All she does is sit in her office all day and fuck up," Lakara said. Her sentiments were right in line with many of the staff members, students, and parents' feelings about the school and the district.

"Just cause she's that way, that doesn't give you the right to act the way you do. Come on, Lakara—" Travis vented while putting his face in his hands, revving up to say more.

"And why do you act that way?" I interrupted Travis, who was about to go off on a tirade. I couldn't stand it anymore, so I stopped writing, turned around, and faced everyone.

"You come in here thinking that fight yesterday is cool. You're talking like that is your livelihood. Lakara, your livelihood should be those books and succeeding in life. You come to me all the time asking to get placed in your right grade, but you guys aren't doing the things you need to do to progress," I said. "Getting into fights, especially like the one that happened yesterday, is definitely not helping you move forward. Travis is right. Fights like the one yesterday are giving our people a bad name. You're a young lady, and you have to portray yourself as such. You cannot go out there fighting at the drop of a dime. One day it is going to lead you to a situation you can't get out of."

"Williams, I just got a lot of anger inside me," Lakara said.

"What? What anger do you have inside you? Tell me. Everyone gets upset. I get angry. Travis, yeah Travis gets angry. You don't see us walking around, knocking people upside their heads and laughing about it. You're using the anger thing as an excuse—"

Lakara interrupted me: "I saw my uncle shoot my father when I was four."

The room fell silent. The expressions on my and Travis' faces were blank. We were speechless. If Lakara had said, "Got nothing to say now, huh?" I still wouldn't have responded, but she didn't make a wise crack. She just told us more as we sat with astonished faces.

"I was sitting next to my father on the couch. He was pretty much in and out of my life. He didn't support me, or my mom. He was a bum, but he would stop by from time to time to see me. My uncle couldn't stand him. He felt like he wasn't a man and didn't take care of what he needed to, so while we were sitting on the couch watchin' TV, he came in with a .45 and shot him in the head."

"While you were sitting there?" Travis asked.

"Yeah! My uncle is a loose cannon. He's in jail now. Not for that, but for somethin' else. For killing someone else, I think. My mother doesn't talk much about it, and why should she?"

"You can still remember it?" I asked, hoping to shed more light.

"It's not crystal clear, but I do have images of the blood dripping down the couch. But that wasn't the last time I saw someone get shot; just the first. Since then, almost every summer I've seen a shooting. Remember I told y'all about that boy that shot another boy down the street from my house?" Her girls nodded in approval. "I couldn't believe it. I was like, 'Did I just see that? Did that boy just stand over him and blow his head off?'" As Lakara talked about the situation, it gave her a rush, and she seemed excited when she turned to her girls to reminisce.

"Did you tell anyone?" Travis asked.

"I ain't no snitch," she said proudly.

"Listen, if you tell someone about something of that magnitude, it does not make you a snitch. You're not a gangster," I said.

"I never said I was no gangster, Williams."

"Then what is all this 'snitching' business?" I demanded.

"I'm just not going to be out here telling on people," she said as she looked down, playing with her hands.

I calmed down and lowered my voice. After finding out that she saw her uncle shoot her father and at such a young age, I felt sorry for her. By the looks of things, Travis was still in a daze, so I had to speak for both of us.

"Slow down, you hear me? Calm down with all this fighting and rage. Try to use your anger to work for you. I hear you are a talented dancer, and I know you can do some hair, too. I see the styles you wear and the hookups you give your girls. All y'all come in dressed sharp as a tack. You come in with your high heels, out of dress code of course, but you're sharp," I said.

Lakara and her crew laughed at my old school terminology. It was a long shot trying to get them to come to school and follow the dress code – a sky blue shirt, dark blue skirt, black stockings, and flat black shoes. I didn't really want to hound them too much after Lakara said what she did, so I tried to find something positive to say, "Look, you guys have to get back to class. You can't be using my office as a cutting spot. Get out of here and use that creativity. I'll mess around and see you on TV one day or something," I said.

As they walked out, I told Lakara that she could come in and talk whenever she was feeling stressed and to avoid anymore incidents like the one that had happened the day before. "All right, Mr. Williams," she said.

"That girl ain't gonna change," Travis said, leaning back in his chair.

"I know, but I wouldn't be doing my job if I just sat through all that and said nothing."

"Oh no, brother, you did what you were supposed to do, but she ain't gonna change. She's doomed. She is too into the street life. Her uncle shot her father, and she saw it. Damn. No wonder she is such a problem."

"Yeah," I said, sighing for Lakara.

"Speaking of crazy, we had to search the kids this morning in the auditorium before we let them come upstairs," Travis tried to break the stillness with exciting, but bad, news.

"Did you find anything?"

"Officer Caroll and I were on stage standing with two officers. One of the officers was telling the students how the search was going to go. He said, 'Everyone line up on this side of the stairs. Come on the stage, and you will be searched one by one. Then exit on the other side of the stage stairs and head to class. If a weapon or anything illegal is found on a person, they will not be allowed to exit, and we will deal with them.'"

"Did anyone get in trouble?"

"One guy did, a sixth grader. They found a knife on him, but everyone else was smart."

"What do you mean?"

"After the students left the auditorium, Caroll and I were getting ready to go down to our office when she noticed something sticking out of one of the isles. It was a razor. So we searched the isles, and we found all types of stuff—weed, knives, razors, everything but a gun."

"That's a shame—weapons and drugs. I still can't believe all those people out there fighting," I said, still stuck on what happened the day before. "Parents! They should have been out there to make sure nothing happened, not to make sure that something did."

"I was the only person out there who was trying to stop the fight, and Matthews and Gladstone were nowhere around."

"You should have known they weren't going to be out there. Things happen in the building, and they don't do anything. I can't count the number of times I've seen a child run away before they could get to an incident. All the kids have to hear is, 'Here comes Matthews,' or, 'Here comes Gladstone,' and they break for it."

"They don't pay me enough for this," Travis complained. "I could have gotten killed yesterday. I'll never do nothing like that again."

"It's like 11:30. Y'all been in here all morning talking," Officer Caroll said through the door. I opened the door and let her in. "That Lakara is a rude bitch. She was all the way down at the other end of the hallway. I tell her to go to class, and you know what she tells me?"

"What?" Travis and I asked simultaneously.

"'Shut the fuck up.' If I was younger and not so heavy, I would have chased her ass down," Caroll said, chuckling.

Travis and I sat there shaking our heads, thinking about how Lakara had just left the room and she was back at it already, acting a fool.

"What?" Caroll asked.

"Nothing," Travis responded. "You hear anymore about the weapons downstairs? What happened to the boy with the knife?" he changed topics.

"They took him down to the station, and his parents are going to pick him up down there."

"Oh well, might as well add him to the mob of students and parents that were taken down to the station in that wagon yesterday," Travis said.

Travis didn't say any more, because Caroll and her loud mouth were in the room. Besides, he was still angry at her for being nowhere to be found during the crisis.

"Oh yeah! What happened? I heard yesterday was crazy. Uh, I had to take my son to the doctor," Caroll said coming up with a quick excuse for why she wasn't there.

"Yeah, it was crazy," Travis said, slightly flustered. He turned his head in the opposite direction, sickened by Caroll's presence.

Officer Caroll sensed the tension. She changed the topic again, "Yeah, these parents are crazy. Hey, Williams, did you ever tell Travis about the mother who came into the school police office the other day?"

"No, I forgot to tell him," I said.

Chafie Fields

"Last week Caroll, Farell, and I were sitting in the school police office," I said. "I came in looking for you, but you didn't come in that day. While the three of us were sitting in there, two officers came in." I told Travis the rest of the story:

"Can I help you?" Caroll said to the officers.

"Yeah, we're looking for Chafie Fields."

"Why?" she asked.

"We received a complaint that the gym teacher was harassed by a student."

"By who?" Caroll asked as she got out of her chair and grabbed her handcuffs, in route to the gym.

They came back to the office about ten minutes later, and Chafie's mother was right behind them with her boyfriend.

She was very dramatic. She was 45 years old, but she looked about 57, and she complained about her heart whenever Chafie was in trouble.

"'Oh—oh—oh!" Chafie's mother moaned as she held her chest.

"Are you okay, miss?" one of the officers asked. Officer Caroll put her arm around the woman's shoulder in concern.

I stayed put, sitting at Ellway's old desk. Something just didn't feel right about Chafie's mother.

"Oh—I can't take it. I can't take this," Chafie's mother whined, holding her chest tighter and tighter. I didn't know if she was referring to her chest pain or the thought of her son going to jail.

The office phone rang. Caroll answered it. "Hello? Are you sure, Mr. Burton?" She hung up the phone. "All right! The gym teacher isn't going to press any charges."

Suddenly, Chafie's mother had a burst of energy, "Wait until I see him. I'm gonna kill Chafie!" She was no longer holding her chest, and appeared full of vigor and determination. She was trying to show that she was a strong parent and that Chafie didn't need the police to teach him a lesson because she was going to take care of everything.

"Where is Chafie, anyway?" Farell asked from her seat at the coffee table.

"Yeah, good question, Farell," Caroll said.

"We've been looking for him all over the school, and we have come up empty-handed. He must have run out of the building after he pushed and spit on Mr. Burton, and told him he was going to kill him."

"Is he one of the eighth graders?" I asked.

"No, he's 11. He's in the sixth grade," his mother responded with an angry look on her face, forgetting all about her heart problem. "I know exactly where he is, and I'm going to wear his little tail out." She paused. "So, I guess y'all are done, huh?"

"Yeah, Ms. Fields. If the teacher doesn't want to press charges, and Mrs. Matthews doesn't want to press charges, and she never does, then I guess we can go."

As the police were about to walk out of the office, the gym teacher came in. "You know what?" he said. "I think I am going to press charges. I'm tired of being disrespected."

"Oh—oh—oh!" Miss Field's heart pain started again. "I can't take it," she said, holding her chest.

"Do you have any pills, Miss Fields?" Caroll suggested.

"I left them at the house, officer. Oh—oh!"

"Who is this?" asked Mr. Burton.

"Miss Fields, Chafie's mom," Caroll responded.

Miss Fields' sympathy act must have worked because Mr. Burton started to soften up.

"Well—well, uh, all right, I guess I'll drop the charges, but tell your son—wait, where *is* Chafie?"

"He ran out of the building, and I'm gonna find him. Yeah! Uh-huh," Miss Fields answered with spunk as she reached her hand out and put it on his shoulder.

"Yeah, because Chafie has to follow rules and understand that he can't always do what he wants to, you know?" Mr. Burton said, taking a handkerchief and wiping his face where the spit used to be.

"I know, and Chafie will know when I wear his tail out. I'm going to kill him," Miss Fields said. She strained her voice, and I assumed she was trying to keep us from catching on to her scam. It was too late for that. In my eyes, it was amateur night, and I could see right through her act. Any speculation of her son going to jail meant it was time to fake heart trouble.

"Now, ain't that somethin'?" Travis said. He leaned back in his chair and put his hands on his head. "These parents have absolutely no shame. You know why that boy spit in the gym teacher's face when Mr. Burton was giving him those instructions? Because he has no rules at home," Travis said, answering his own question. "Mr. Burton is a damn fool if you ask me. He should have pressed charges until that bitch dropped dead because as far as I'm concerned, she is useless."

Caroll started laughing hysterically; she liked to know she wasn't the only angry person at the school.

"I don't know what the world is coming to. Parents are out here faking heart attacks to keep the children out of prison instead of raising them right from the beginning," I said. "She should have let the police find her son and spend a night down there at the station. He probably would have straightened out then." I leaned back in my chair.

"That's what Charles's father did," Travis said.

"You mean Chafie."

"No, my brother. Charles. The eighth grader."

"You talkin' about the grown ass man Charles from the eighth grade? The one Marlow sent out on the court to hurt us in the student-staff basketball game?" I asked.

"Yeah, his pop let him stay in jail," Travis responded with a smile on his face. Charles had taken his shirt off while trying to fight a school police officer. He had also called himself a "grown ass man" in the student-staff game that his team was losing, when he bumped shoulders with Travis and almost made him lose his cool.

"What happened that day, anyway?" I asked.

"After school, over on Allen Street— Charles was outside with no shirt on in mid-March, talking that grown ass man shit again. He was about to fight three boys from Arsen High. Cleveland and his crew got to the scene the same time I did.

"The middle of Allen? Weren't you supposed to be outside anyway?"

"I had some paperwork to do. I'm on the job, though. I'm on the job. You know I'm the top cop," we started laughing.

Caroll could see that she was being edged out of the conversation, so she excused herself. "All right, y'all, I'm going downstairs."

"All right," Travis and I replied as the door closed.

"Caroll wasn't anywhere to be found during this incident either, was she?" I asked.

"You know she wasn't," Travis responded, shaking his head. "So this fool was outside with no shirt on, pacing back and forth, balling up his fists, and flexing his little ass chest. Talking about, 'I'm a grown ass man, I'm a grown ass man, dog.' But there was no fight. Cleveland cleared the street, and we took Charles into the school police office."

"Good, then you guys took care of business," I said.

"But Cleveland confiscated his bag because he heard a rumor that Charles had a gun in school. Cleveland looked inside the bag and found an automatic pistol with an infrared on top."

"The gun had an infrared on it? Yeah, right." I was shocked that a child would carry such a sophisticated gun to school.

"Good brother, I'm serious."

"What did Cleveland do when he found the gun?"

"He couldn't do anything at first because Charles put the bag down outside to take off his shirt. They say since he placed the bag down outside, someone else could have put the gun in there."

"That's ridiculous. Well, I guess not—too much doubt, huh?" I asked, thinking out loud.

"Yeah, until Cleveland called his house. Come to find out, the boy stole the gun from his father, and his father let Cleveland take the boy down to the station. All I know is that Charles wasn't talking all that grown ass man shit then. He was a quiet ass man getting into the back of Cleveland's car. I think his father let him stay down there overnight, but I'm not sure. I haven't seen him since that incident."

"You know what? I'm starting to put all this together. I think Mrs. Matthews actually had him removed from the school," I said as I wrote in my records. I stopped talking and lifted my head up to crack my neck. I saw Miss Helen peeking in the window.

"Let me in, Williams. I need to use your phone." This was the nosiest but most resourceful teacher at Parish Hill. She knew all the rules, and the ones she didn't know, she made up. The only thing she knew more about than the rules was gossip.

"What y'all talkin' 'bout?" she asked, stepping into my office, filling it with attitude. She had on a white blouse, tiger patterned capris, and red pumps, and she had blonde microbraids. She stood there with her hand on her hip, looking at Travis and me like we better answer her or else. Travis looked at me.

"Helen, do you know what happened to Charles?" I asked. "He was one of your students, right?"

"Charles' crazy ass doesn't go here anymore. He got kicked out for that gun thing. Y'all didn't know that?"

"Yeah, well, we weren't sure. You know, we just wanted to check."

"Matthews sent out a letter to all the students' parents stating that Charles had been thrown out of the school for the gun possession so the kids would feel safe," she explained. "Now, can I use your phone?"

"Yeah, sure. Go ahead."

"Thanks. Y'all can keep talking," she said, sitting down at the table near Travis.

I kept working on my records, and Travis sat there quietly. We were both on the same page; we weren't going to talk anymore until she left the room. It was the only thing that made sense because even if we wanted to talk, we wouldn't be able to hear ourselves over Helen. She was screaming and cursing at whoever was on the phone.

"Yeah, uh huh, uh huh—see that's that bullshit. Well, you just make sure everything goes right next time, motherfucker. Yeah, mm hm. Make sure it goes right next time, fucking bastard." She hung up the phone. "All right, y'all. I'll talk to you later. Thanks, Williams."

"All right, Helen." We both acknowledged her leaving.

"You see, now that's what these girls have to follow as role models. They can turn on the tube and see women half-dressed, or up close and personal, *that* is what they deal with—cursing, loud dressing, tacky nonsense like what just stormed out of here," I said.

"Hey, brother, there *were* a lot of parents that resembled her yesterday. Some of those ladies had on high heels and were out there hittin' other parents and children with fake Louis Vuitton purses."

"You know what's really sad, Travis?"

"What?"

"Helen has a 10-year-old daughter."

"That's a shame," Travis looked down at the floor shaking his head. Just then, we heard a loud bang and a bunch of yelling. Travis jumped up and looked out the office door window. Lakara was coming, with officer Caroll right behind her.

"Williams! Williams!" Lakara yelled, knocking on the door. "Tell her I just came from here."

"I don't care! You need to take your little black ass to class," Caroll yelled back.

"Come on, y'all, relax," Travis had opened the door and was trying to calm them down.

I peeked my head around to see both Lakara and Caroll. "Lakara, you came from here an hour ago."

"Williams, you're drawn, man," Lakara said because I didn't back up her claim.

"Lakara, what do you want me to do? Lie? You left here an hour ago. You have to go to class."

"Yeah, whatever. Hey, yo, Kyle, what's up?" Lakara turned up the hallway to find an excuse.

"What's up, Lakara? How are you?" Mr. Kyle replied, giving Lakara the break she needed to just walk away and return to class on her own. Mr. Kyle was partially scared of Lakara, so it wasn't surprising that he allowed this to happen.

"Hey, Kyle, that girl needs to be in class. Kyle!" Officer Caroll yelled, still irate.

"All right, baby girl, what class are you supposed to be in?" Mr. Kyle said delicately. But it set Lakara off.

"Man, y'all drawn, man," Lakara yelled back as she stormed down the hallway and turned the corner.

"Yeah, and you better be goin' to my room, too. If I don't see you in there, you know what it's gonna be," Kyle said, putting on a third floor lead teacher show in front of us. He turned around, looked at us, and shrugged his shoulders.

"Look at Kyle standing in the hallway with his hands on his hips acting like he did something," I said.

Caroll and Travis broke out into laughter as they walked back to my office.

"What was that?" Kyle asked, looking in our direction, acting tough. The office door closed, and his voice became inaudible.

"That guy is such a clown," Travis laughed, and Caroll and I agreed.

"But Lakara is a menace. That girl is going to end up dead. Her mother needs to raise her better than that," Caroll stated, not knowing the history lesson that Travis and I endured an hour ago.

Mrs. Matthews called for Caroll on the walkie talkie: "Officer Caroll? Officer Caroll, are you there? Come in please."

"Damn! That's the third time today. She cracks me up how she is all polite sounding. She's probably calling me to give me a duty that is going to break my back while she sits in her office chillin' all day. How come she couldn't call you?" Caroll gestured in Travis' direction. She snatched the walkie talkie off her hip and tried to sound as professional as she possibly could, "Yes, Mrs. Matthews?"

"I need you to come down to my office. There is something I need to show you."

"In route," Caroll snapped. "Damn! She is always calling me." She stormed out of my office, tussling with the door and pushing it as hard as she could like a child who got called in the house for supper too early.

"That's 'cause you're always kissing her ass," Travis said under his breath, but Caroll didn't hear him. "She has some nerve to be talking about parenting. Her son ain't no model citizen, either. He comes to work with her pretty often."

"Yeah, I know," I said. "He is always walking right behind her or hanging out in the office with y'all."

"Well, that boy is fucked up. He was trying to fuck one of those eighth grade girls. I think he succeeded."

"What would he want with the girls at this school?" I asked Travis. "He's nineteen and goes to community college. He's like 6'5" or 6'6", one or two inches taller than I am."

"Yeah, that's why I don't even say anything when she starts talking about parents and these kids, because I know how her shit is. I got nothing to say to her. Especially after that shit she pulled yesterday, leaving me out to dry during the brawl." Travis was still releasing frustration; I wanted to know more about her son.

"Yo, how do you know about her son trying to mess with these little girls?"

"Ellway told me. I talked to him on the phone the other day."

"How is he?"

"He's all right. He asked if Caroll was still letting her son come up here and told me to be careful."

"I knew something was fishy about that kid." I remembered more. "Caroll is always talking about taking him to the doctor—the boy is nineteen and in college. I remember being in the school police office when she was saying she had to leave early to take her son to the doctor. He was sitting their like a four-year-old with his hands folded, resting his head on top of them, looking up trying to get some sympathy. I figured Caroll told him to put on that act so that she could get out of work early."

"See, Caroll ain't right. Not only is her son trying to play mack daddy with the young jawns, but she is using him to help in her scams. Come to think of it, one of the young jawns came in the office looking for his silly ass. I wouldn't be the least bit surprised if he got her pregnant." Travis sat and crossed his arms.

"That's not just bad parenting, that's no parenting," I said.

"What do you mean, good brother?"

"I don't think he has a father around. I think Caroll is raising him alone."

"She has raised him alone. That's a good point, my brother. She was, just the other day, talking about how her mother buys all his clothes and that's who they live with."

"But Travis, it's not always the buying or economics. A lot of the time, it's about morals."

"You're right, you're right." I could tell Travis was really thinking about what I was saying.

"These kids need to be taught about higher expectations. They need a dose of pride or something, and the parents seem to be a poor source. That shit we witnessed yesterday, Caroll and her bullshit, parents like Helen, these are the poor sources. My father wasn't the richest man in the world—in fact, he was poor as hell—but you know what he does now?"

"What?" Travis asked.

"He's an attorney. I'm not saying these kids have to be lawyers, but not many of them are going to be able to say they achieved their dreams, because they never tried, and they certainly weren't given the proper guidance. The only person who actually believed in my father was his mother, God rest her soul. You know what? Poor may be an understatement for what my father was, but he used that—the anger and frustrations of being poor and people telling him he couldn't become an attorney—to succeed."

"Good brother, your father is a legend and an exception."

"You know what? We need more exceptions, then. We need more of these youngsters to have common sense. If my father hadn't reached his goal, he would have done *something* positive. You know why? Because he had a good head on his shoulders. He would fight sometimes, but he got good grades. He had respect for people and wanted to live. Half the children here don't care whether they live or die, like Lakara. If you don't care whether you live or die, if you don't respect yourself, how are you going to respect anyone else, let alone get good marks in school?"

"You know what, brother? That fight yesterday basically summed up Lakara's life and every kid like hers: hell in a hand basket."

Travis was right. It seemed that everyone at Parish Hill was on a chaotic road to failure. And after spending almost an entire school year at Parish Hill, it was obvious to me that the parents and staff were leading the way.

Still Going

Tyreak was allowed to come back to Parish Hill, even after he terrorized Ms. Wilson. I did not know whether it was Matthew's decision or whether an official at the school district made the call and refused to place Tyreak at another school, but Matthews and Gladstone took the blame for it around Parish Hill. Nothing changed about Tyreak's behavior. He came back and committed the same stupid acts. He was still yelling, playing, cutting class, and throwing anything within reach.

Tyreak did not care about himself, and he did not care about others. If anything, Tyreak wanted to see others fail because his future was dim and bleak. Misery loves company, and he was misery if I ever came across it. Almost 17 in the seventh grade, he was at the point of no return. There was no getting a child like this back. He wasn't even trying to be successful. Success to him was watching other people fail alongside him. If he could witness this at the end of his day, he was content.

Worst of all, Tyreak was the epitome of the word punk. I never saw him pick on someone who would fight him back; it was always a teacher because teachers weren't allowed to get physical, one of the seventh grade boys who he knew was afraid of him, or a girl.

Tyreak's encounter with Denise Jenkins was the most extreme case of him picking on a girl. Kushner brought it to my attention, so I looked into it.

Denise Jenkins came across as a little eccentric. There were tons of rumors circulating about her, and it made it hard for me to look into the situation with an open mind. I stepped out of my office and ran into the hall monitor who knows all.

"Hey, Willy!"

"What's up, Jay?" Willy replied. He was concentrating on the halls to make sure every kid was in class.

"Yo, man, I need to talk to you about Denise."

"What about her?"

"Is she being sexually harassed?"

"By who?" he asked.

"By Tyreak Jones?"

"Hey, Jay, you know what? She is, but guess what? It's for a reason."

"What's the reason?"

"Jay, Denise is not the little sweet girl she wants people to think she is. She is very much sexually active."

"Really?" I said, raising an eyebrow. Denise was only 14.

"Yeah," Willy replied, sitting down in his chair. "Jay, she has the eighth graders coming to the floor looking for her. They will be like 'Yo, where's the jawn Denise at? I'm tryin' to get my man ate.'"

"Willy, they come up here and say that to you?"

"Yup, they come up here looking for her so they can get blow jobs, but I don't even act amazed. I just send them back down to the second floor. Jay, she worked hard for this reputation. I have seen boys look at me and then look at her, then look back at me, and wipe the side of their face, if you know what I mean."

"Well look, man, it was reported to me that Tyreak Jones has been sexually harassing her, so I have to check it out," I said, walking away.

"I know what that's about!" Willy blurted out.

I stopped in my tracks and turned and looked at Willy, "You know what what's about?"

"I know why Tyreak and Larry are giving Denise problems."

"I never said anything about Tyreak's crony, Larry. I just said Tyreak." He looked the other way, not wanting to give me any more information. I felt like a detective trying to pry information out of a suspect who didn't want to snitch.

"Willy, tell me!"

Willy said nothing.

"You know what, forget it. I'm gone," I said, walking towards Denise's classroom. I was frustrated; Willy was acting like one of the kids.

"Denise already did it," Willy blurted out.

"Did what?" I asked, turning around once again.

"Denise hooked them up and gave them slob jobs. Now they want her to do it again, and she doesn't want to, so they are giving her a hard time."

"This situation is out of control. I don't even feel the least bit comfortable handling this one. Shit!" I realized that I was complaining unnecessarily to Willy, and I stopped immediately. "All right, I'm going to check on this. I'll talk to you later."

"Hey, Jay, who put you onto this?"

"Who do you think?" I replied as I walked by Mr. Kushner's room and gestured at the door.

"That's fucked up! His fat ass is always bitchin'," Willy said, siding with the kids and making light of a situation I felt was very serious.

He was verbalizing what a lot of people felt at Parish Hill - that if a student didn't report it or a teacher didn't witness it, then it didn't happen. That went for everything except suicide notes. The only reason we acted on those was because of another incident, which had turned principal Matthews into a nervous wreck. Willy might have thought this was just extra work for me, but it was my job, plus I hated when boys took advantage of girls.

"Excuse me, Ms. Gertrude, may I speak to Denise, please?"

"You certainly may. Please, take her off my hands. Her behavior has been outrageous all morning. She's been running around class yelling and screaming at the top of her lungs that I'm a redneck."

Ms. Gertrude was an old-fashioned, Caucasian woman. She had been teaching at Parish Hill for four years, and it was still hard for her to digest the fact that kids have a difficult time sitting still, being patient, learning, and doing what they are told.

As she complained to me, I had to hold my breath because I did not want her strong perfume scent to set off my allergies.

"Mr. Williams, she has been calling us niggers and monkeys!" Denise said in her defense. I stepped a bit further inside so the class would feel my presence and settle down a little.

"Denise, settle down. What is this on the blackboard?" I asked Ms. Gertrude, amazed at what I was reading.

"These are the rude, offensive names they accused me of calling them, so I wrote them on the blackboard," she claimed, her third chin shaking back and forth.

"No, these are the names she called us," Denise said. The class erupted in agreement.

"Everyone settle down and stop playing," I shouted. I took Denise out of the classroom before she started a race riot. "How are you feeling?"

"Fine, Mr. Williams," she said with a smile on her face.

"None of these boys have been bothering you in any way?"

"No, Mr. Williams. Why are you asking me all these questions?" she asked, still smiling, clueless as to what I was talking about.

I thought of three possibilities: Maybe she was too scared to tell me, but that was not like Denise. Maybe she really didn't know what I was talking about and both Kushner and Willy were off their rockers. Or maybe she knew exactly what I was talking about and didn't want to tell me because she didn't want to be labeled a snitch.

After unsuccessfully trying to get Denise to divulge, I let her go back to the classroom and prayed that Ms. Gertrude could attain some type of order. I had a feeling that she was in that classroom calling those children out of their names, but I just made a mental note of it. I had heard that Ms. Gertrude and another Caucasian teacher at the school called the students racist names. The administration knew about the problem, but it was swept under the rug like so many other problems at Parish Hill.

I walked down the hallway to my office, and Willy was sitting in front of it. "No luck, huh?"

"Nope. She didn't want to be a snitch."

"I could have told you that," Willy said, wiping his head with his towel.

"These kids are too concerned with trying to be cool and tough." I shook my head, frustrated.

"Hey, Jay, you ain't gonna get nothing out of these kids. Not if they don't want you to."

"Yeah, but they act like they are on the street or something, like they are part of a gang. It's crazy. I tell them all the time, if you tell a teacher or any adult in the building about a situation, then you're doing what you are supposed to do."

"Yeah, but a lot of these kids aren't trying to hear that."

"Who cares what they're trying to hear? "

After leaving Willy, I pulled the keys out of my pocket, unlocked my office door, went inside, and sat at my desk, trying to shake my irritation. I couldn't get past how Willy was acting like a child.

After answering calls and meeting with students, I realized it was time to cover a class. I gathered my stuff, and I was off to room 307, Ms. Gertrude's room. She needed to leave in the middle of the day for a doctor's appointment. I wouldn't be surprised if she just wanted to escape the turmoil she had created earlier.

When I walked into the class, Denise and Tyreak were in there. They were at each other's throats the entire time.

"Stop throwing stuff at me, Tyreak!" Denise shouted at him.

"I didn't throw nothing at you."

Ms. Gertrude didn't leave any work for the class in her absence, and since I was not a teacher, I had nothing. In situations like that, I usually talked to the class about something constructive or let them sit and talk amongst themselves. Tyreak took full advantage of that. Whenever he felt as though I wasn't looking, he threw something at Denise. I missed the first time he did it, but I did not miss the second.

"Tyreak!" I said after a pen had just missed the side of Denise's face. "Do not throw anything again. Stop playing around. Get your act together." I put my head down to do some more work. It couldn't have been more than 10 seconds, and Denise exploded.

"Y'all gonna stop playin' with me!" Denise picked up a desk, walked it across the room, and threw it at Tyreak. He quickly dodged before she let it go.

"Both of you get over here!" I pulled them out into the hallway and told Ms. Davis, the hall monitor on duty at the time, to watch Tyreak while I talked to Denise.

"You better not snitch, Denise! You hear me, bitch? You better not snitch, or I am going to beat you the fuck up," Tyreak screamed.

I ignored him and looked for my office key. Ms. Davis was not so quiet. "Hey, Tyreak, close your mouth now!" she said forcefully. I was not surprised when Tyreak listened to her. Ms. Davis was slowly receiving the respect she deserved from the children.

I'd seen her in action before. One day before classes started, there was nothing but teachers on the third floor preparing the classrooms and getting ready for the seventh graders to come up the steps. But one of the students had snuck upstairs to the third floor, and when Ms. Davis saw him walking into one of the classrooms, she confronted him. "Get out of there, Karl, and let Ms. Hamilton get her day started."

"Yeah, get the hell out of my room, you little heathen, so I can get ready for the rest of your buddies to come up here," Ms. Hamilton chimed in.

"Why? I don't want to leave. I want to stay up here," his high-pitched voice was killing my ears as I looked down the hallway to take in the action.

"Why you want to stay up here?" Ms. Davis asked.

"I just do."

"Well, that answer ain't good enough!" Ms. Davis replied.

"I'm stayin' up here," Karl whined back.

"No, you're not. Get your ass back downstairs," Ms. Davis demanded as she pushed Karl.

"Why you gotta put your hands on me though?"

"Because that's the only thing that works with y'all, you dumb motherfucker." She followed up the push with a smack to the back of Karl's head.

"What the fuck, man?"

Ms. Davis then put the whining little boy in a headlock while preaching: "What? I'm tired of you little bastards asking questions and not doing what you're supposed to do. When a grown-up tells you to do something, just shut your mouth and do what you're told! Now take your little stupid ass downstairs, Karl!" She let him go and gave him a push in the direction of the stairs. He went in silence with his lip poked out.

I wasn't the only person who remembered; Tyreak did as well, and he did not reply to Ms. Davis because he didn't want to get physically embarrassed in return.

Once Denise and I were inside my office, I played detective. "What happened, Denise? Tell me now. Has Tyreak been teasing you?"

"Yeah."

"Now, why couldn't you tell me that when I asked you before? What is he teasing you about?" I questioned.

"He keeps askin' me to suck his dick."

"How long has this been going on?"

"Since the beginning of school," she confessed.

"Wait, this has been going on since September?"

"Yeah."

"How come you didn't tell anyone? Why haven't you told a teacher, an officer, or me?" She shrugged her shoulders.

"Well, it's in my hands now, and we are going downstairs to the school police."

"What are we going to tell them?" she asked nervously.

"We have to tell them about the sexual harassment that has been going on," I said. "We also have to tell them that Tyreak threatened you."

School Police Office

"Who's at the door?" Ellway asked as he tried to look through the window to see who it was.

"It's Williams," I responded.

"Yo, what's up Williams?"

"What's up, Ellway?" He was back in the building more regularly now that his previous issue had been resolved.

"Why do you have Denise with you?" he asked, as if he knew she was in trouble or giving me a hard time.

"Well, she was just threatened by Tyreak, and he has been sexually harassing her, too."

"Did you see Tyreak threaten her?"

"Yes, I did."

"What? You were standing there?"

"Yes, I was trying to get into my office, and he shouted over Miss Davis and me."

"What did he say?"

"He said that if she told me anything, he was going to beat her the F-up," I said, leaning closer to Ellway.

"Is that what he said?" Ellway asked, looking at Denise with sincere concern. Denise just nodded her head and poked out her lip, trying to suck up as much of the sympathy as she possibly could.

"Williams, let me talk to you out in the hallway for a minute," Ellway said with a stern face. "Honey, just relax in here while we step out in the hallway to talk for a minute." Ellway reached his hand out to Denise to comfort her.

She nodded her head again, made a puppy dog face, and took a seat.

Once we were out in the hallway, I was Jay again.

"Jay, there are two sides to this sword."

"Ellway, I know, I know, I have that feeling. I have the feeling that Denise has done something, also. But I saw Tyreak threaten Denise—right outside my office. I saw it with my own eyes. I am going to write up what I heard and saw on a pink slip and put it in your hands because that is what we have to do."

"You're right, Jay, but you know she is lying right?"

"Hey man, that may be, but we have to protect every kid's safety. I heard the threat, and that is what I am going to write down and hand to you. I have also written down the complaints she has about being sexually harassed. If she complains to you while you guys are in there talking, then write down whatever she says so that this whole thing doesn't fall back into your lap."

"Jay, I know what I have to do, but I just hate helping a kid that is as bad as Denise."

"I know Denise is not as sweet as she tries to come across, but Tyreak is just as nasty or worse, and he is the one who is making the threats."

"You know what, Jay? Some of these girls deserve that shit. They need their asses whipped."

"Yo, man I don't play that. There is no need for a man to be hitting on a girl," I said.

"Sometimes there is."

"Ellway, you have a daughter. What about her?" I asked, in an attempt to get him on my page.

"That's different."

"Why?"

"Because, if anyone touches my daughter, I'll whip their ass."

"Man, you ain't shit. You know where I am going with this. Look, make sure you write down whatever she says, and after you're done talking, send her upstairs to my office. I'll be up there writing down what I heard. I'll give you and Gladstone copies when I'm done."

"All right, bet," Ellway replied.

We gave each other a handshake and a hug and went back to work.

After Denise talked to Ellway, she was back at my door. "So did you tell him everything?"

"Yeah!" she said with an attitude.

I ignored the anger. "All right, good. Is there anything else you want to talk about?"

"No."

"Now if you feel unsafe in anyway, or he actually does something, then let me or Officer Ellway know."

"Okay," she answered, with very little confidence that anyone in the school cared about her safety. I had a sense that something wasn't right, but I tried to keep it positive as I rushed her out of my office; I had to get ready for a parent meeting.

"All right, it's 2:45. What do you have now?"

"What?" she asked, confused. I could tell that her mind was not on class.

"What class do you have, sweetheart? It's the last period of the day."

"I have gym."

"I'll write you a pass so the teacher doesn't mark you late or think you were cutting."

I gave her the pass, and she was off. I couldn't shake that bad feeling. I remembered the angry look on Tyreak's face when he shouted at Denise. I thought of the force that he could direct towards her, and I knew she was in trouble. The only way to stop him from getting to her was to have a personal bodyguard at her side at all times.

I knew that whatever happened, it would be upsetting, but the administration's follow-up would be an even bigger disappointment. I had seen Ellway do his job, and he was pretty efficient, but everything had to go through Mrs. Matthews and Ms. Gladstone, and that was where the process seemed to get botched.

The end of the day came before I could blink my eyes. I left exhausted.

The next day, I came into school still tired.

Ms. Davis was right on my heels as I entered my office. "Mr. Williams, did you hear about what happened yesterday?"

"No. What happened?" I asked eagerly, hoping it had nothing to do with Denise. "He hit her," Ms. Davis said.

I'd known it was coming, but I was still surprised. I gritted my teeth and balled up my fists, disturbed by the news. "How did it happen?" I asked.

"Well, he met her outside, walked up to her, and hit her on the jaw. I mean, he hit her hard, too. She fell."

"She fell down? Was she crying?"

"No, she wasn't crying. She took it, but she fell, and after a few minutes, she got up."

"Did he knock her out?"

"No, she just sat there in a daze and gathered herself, got up, and began to walk home. I stood there behind her and kept asking her if she was okay while she sat on the ground. Every time I would ask her if she was okay, she just said, 'Yes.'"

I wondered if Denise would be in school that day. I hadn't seen her outside on my way in, but it was still a little early. I wanted to see if she was okay. There were supposed to be school police outside after school making sure no fights broke out. After I attended to some business with parents and a social worker, I ran downstairs. I banged on the school police office door like a madman.

"Damn, Jay! Why you bangin' on the door like you got a mouse stuck up your ass?" Ellway said as he opened the door.

"Yo, man, what happened with Denise yesterday?" I asked, confident Ellway and the other officers would know what had happened.

"What's going on, my good brother?" Officer Travis asked, coming over and giving me a handshake and a hug because we hadn't seen each other in a while.

"Nothing, man. How you been?"

Before I could ask my question again, Officer Caroll interrupted, "Hey, Williams? Can you believe that ya boy has men calling here for him?"

"What are you talking about?" I asked.

"Yo, he actually has men calling here for him. This dude, Norman, keeps callin' here, askin' to speak to Ellway. He says, 'Hello? Is this the school police office? I have to speak to Officer Ellway, it's urgent.' Ha, ha, ha. Now if you call here and it ain't about business, and every time you call, you need to speak to someone urgently, something is going on. I don't know what to tell you," Officer Caroll said laughing at her own joke as she always did.

"Fuck you, Caroll!" Ellway snapped, as she kept laughing. Travis just sat at his desk shaking his head and grinning.

"What happened with Denise yesterday, y'all?" I asked again.

"What situation with Denise, Jay? I thought that we handled that yesterday," Ellway responded.

"I'm talking about what Tyreak did to her after school," I said on my last breath, tired of the comedy hour.

"Oh, yeah, Tyreak hit her yesterday," Ellway said nonchalantly.

"Did y'all see it?"

"No, Ms. Davis did. She told us about it, but Ms. Gladstone handled the matter herself."

"How come you guys didn't arrest him?"

"Denise didn't want to press any charges, and all Gladstone did was suspend him again."

"That's fucking bullshit!"

"Hey, Jay, why you getting' so hyped?"

"Because I'm sick of this school. It's ridiculous. Kids keep acting up and nothing ever happens to them. All they get is a dumb-ass suspension. Ms. Gladstone and Mrs. Matthews have a hard time keeping order in this school because all they do is sit in their offices and give orders to people on those walkie talkies. When a parent comes into the school, they call my extension, or whoever else they can grab, for assistance. Tyreak should be gone, out of the school or in some type of correctional facility. He's damn near 18 anyway."

"But the sad thing is, Tyreak got suspended for something else," Ellway said. I knew what he meant – Tyreak could not technically be suspended for punching Denise because he had already been suspended that day, before he punched her. He was only in school because he could not be sent home to what might be an empty house. That was Tyreak's trademark, and it was the second time he had committed a criminal offense while on suspension.

"I have wanted to arrest Tyreak for a long time, but when Denise's guardian doesn't want to press any charges, and the school doesn't want any charges pressed—" Ellway took a deep breath and sighed. He didn't even finish his statement. He just put his hands in the air, shook his head, and stared out the window.

I was outraged. Tyreak should have been arrested. If Mrs. Matthews and Ms. Gladstone weren't going to be the ones to do it, then Denise's parents should have taken the initiative. But maybe there was a reason that Denise said nothing; maybe there was a reason she was able to take that punch.

Months Later

"Mr. Williams."

"Yes, Mrs. Matthews."

"We have an emergency. We need you down here immediately."

"I'm on my way." I hung up the phone and hustled down to the office. When I walked in, I saw a room full of unfamiliar people. They were all visitors, and they were all silent.

"What's going on, Mrs. Matthews?" I asked, thinking I had done something wrong or someone had accused me of doing something I didn't. I nervously gazed at the glum faces around the room.

"Mr. Williams, one of our students committed suicide last night," Mrs. Matthews said, looking down at her twirling thumbs. "He hung himself."

My mouth dropped, and my heart stopped. I waited for Mrs. Matthews to tell me that it was my fault. I expected her to, not because it actually was my fault, but because people at Parish

Hill were always looking to blame someone else for their own failures. I broke out into a mild sweat as I took a seat in the back of the room, but I maintained a calm exterior.

I sat down next to the other black man in the room and realized that his face wasn't unfamiliar after all. He was Jerry Hackleson; I had met him a month earlier when he helped me with CSAP, a program that helped the school district track the progress of academically troubled students. He leaned over to me and started a short rap session while the rest of the office engaged in small talk, "So I see those CSAPs are looking up." He sounded like he was breathing through a respirator.

"Yeah, Jerry, they are. Thanks for all of your help," I whispered back.

"No problem," he said as he wiped the sweat off his forehead and slid back into his seat, his breathing becoming increasingly faint. It made me flashback to the time when he was helping me in my office. We were putting the CSAP information into my computer.

He told me what to do. "All right, make sure you punch in the code first, and then the CSAP form should pop up." After I punched in the information, we waited and waited. The computer was rather slow. When I turned from the screen, I noticed that Jerry had gone to sleep, and, on top of that, he was snoring. He was a large man, which is probably why he breathed heavily and sweated often.

Once the forms showed up on the screen, I tapped him. He woke up and stared at me as if he had no clue who I was or where he was.

To add to the amusement, a fly was buzzing around his head. When it landed on the side of his face, Jerry snapped out of his daze. He shook as if he had the chills and tried to slap the fly.

"Ahh!" Jerry yelled, startled as he missed the fly and hit himself in the face. I acted as if nothing had happened to save him from further embarrassment. Good old Jerry Hackleson. I'll never forget that day he helped me; it more than tripled the CSAPs I had entered on the computer.

He was probably the most sincere school district employee I'd come across, and at that time of crisis, it was good to see him in the room.

"Mr. Williams, are you familiar with Kyree? Kyree Jenkins?" Mrs. Matthews repeated his name.

"No, no I'm not."

"Well, to our knowledge, he hung himself around two or three in the morning. He was a sixth grader in Ms. Cotton's class. Ms. Cotton is crushed." Mrs. Matthews was a nervous wreck. The longer I sat in the room, the clearer things became. The visitors in the room were all members of the crisis team, and Mrs. Matthews was being held under a microscope.

"We should go down to the classrooms and make announcements," a member of the crisis team said.

"What? That's crazy. We can't go to each class and make an announcement about it. Half the students don't know this child," Jerry snapped, disgusted.

"No, no, no. I think we should do it that way so that we personally address each class in the school," the same team member said sternly. Jerry didn't say anything. He ran out of the office to answer his cell phone; members of the crisis team had to answer their phones whenever they rang.

While Jerry was out of the room, the decision was made. The persistent team member spoke his mind some more, and he got his wish. We were going to address each class in the school individually and open a grievance center the next day.

I agreed with Jerry. It was ridiculous to go around to every classroom to talk about the death of a child most students didn't even know, and even more ridiculous to tell them that a grievance center would be open the following day. The students would just use the grievance center to cut class.

The pushy team member said that the same procedure was used at some school out in the suburbs, and it seemed to work. He was missing the point. We were not in a suburban school; we were in an inner city school that was listed as one of the most dangerous schools in the state. By focusing so much attention on the suicide and spending so much time in individual classes, there was a strong possibility that we would end up with more crises to deal with. Many children would envy the attention Kyree was getting.

When Jerry returned to the office, we told him the plan. He sat down and didn't reply. I could sense that mentally and spiritually, Jerry still felt the same way.

As I sat in the tight space, annoyed at the idea of going to the classrooms, someone entered the office and added to my frustration.

"Yes. Allow me to introduce Mr. Marshall. He is our vice principal here at Parish Hill; he joined us about a month ago," Mrs. Matthews said with vigor in her voice, ignoring the fact that he was tardy. Mr. Marshall had come to Parish Hill to assist Mrs. Matthews and Ms. Gladstone with the discipline problems.

As soon as everyone heard "vice principal," they greeted him respectfully. I just stared at him. I wasn't staring because he was the vice principal; Mr. Marshall had brought more than his status as vice principal to Parish Hill – he had also brought trouble.

As he stared back at me and eased into a seat at the table, I remembered a story Willy told me.

"Hey, Willy. Who is the new guy with the receding hair line and beer gut? You know, he looks like he's had a few too many."

"Oh, you're talkin' about Mr. Marshall."

"Is that his name?"

"Yeah. He's the new vice principal. When I first saw him, I thought he was a detective, button-down silk shirt outside his slacks and all."

"He looks like he just came from a bar, had a long night or somethin'."

"Jay, it's funny you said that. From all the gossip I hear about him around here, I think he's a recovering alcoholic. You know we always get the problem folks here at Parish Hill. He lost his job at another school."

"What happened?" I asked.

"I don't know exactly, but I heard that he was removed as principal for disciplinary reasons, and he ended up here."

"That's crazy."

"Who you tellin'? I've seen it all in my seven years here. Nothing surprises me." Willy wiped the sweat off his head with a towel and stared down the hall.

Later, Willy would tell me about the time he had to pull Mr. Marshall and one of the eighth grade girls apart. The girl had accused Mr. Marshall of putting his hands on her and had

Come On Philly, We Can Do Better.

followed him down the hall, right on his back. Willy grabbed the girl, and while Willy was calming her down and walking her back to class, Marshall came up and took a swing at the back of the child's head. Lucky for him, he missed and hit Willy's neck. Marshall and the girl got into fighting position and were about to rumble, but Willy picked up the girl and carried her back to class without speaking to Marshall. Mr. Marshall eventually tried to blame another staff member for a bruise that appeared on the girl's wrist.

Willy said nothing surprised him at Parish Hill, but the look on his face when he talked about Mr. Marshall told me otherwise.

I was still staring at the guy. He was looking back at me, trying to figure out what I was thinking, when a student came into the room and interrupted the meeting, "Mr. Williams, Ms. Gladstone wants to talk to you. She says it's urgent." I looked at Mrs. Matthews, and she gave me the nod to go and see what Ms. Gladstone needed.

On the way to Ms. Gladstone's office, I saw large chunks of weave and ponytails scattered near the entrance. I could only assume there had been a fight between two groups of girls. I had seen it before. I had actually seen girls in Ms. Gladstone's office complaining with their hair in their hands.

I started to hustle, making my way a little bit quicker because I had to be at my assigned classroom, Kyree's homeroom with Ms. Cotton, by 11:30 a.m. It was already ten after.

As I stepped in, I noticed Denise sitting with a slight smirk on her face. She was dressed all in black – black t-shirt, black jeans, and black sneaks. She had her hair pulled back in a ponytail, and it looked extremely greasy. As Denise sat there with a grin on her face, Ms. Gladstone spoke. "Hello, Mr. Williams," she said as if she had just woken up from a nap. "I will assume that you know about everything that is going on."

"Yeah, I do, pretty much. It's a shame," I said shaking my head.

"Yes, it is, Mr. Williams. Denise was Kyree's sister, and her parents brought her to school this morning."

It never crossed my mind that she was related to Kyree, even though they had the same last name.

"Are you okay?" I looked right at Denise.

"Yeah," she responded, still smirking.

Children deal with problems differently, I thought to myself.

"Denise, what do you want to do?" Ms. Gladstone asked her.

"I want to go to class."

"Are you sure? You can go upstairs and talk to Mr. Williams about anything you need to."

"No, I'm okay. I'll be fine," Denise quickly replied.

"Okay," Ms. Gladstone gave her permission to leave, and she headed towards the door.

As she walked out, I told her, "If you need me, you know where to find me."

"Yeah, I know," she replied and kept walking.

"I can't believe that girl's mother brought her to school today," Ms. Gladstone said. She wanted my take on the situation, but I was in a daze, not paying attention to her. I was thinking about Denise Jenkins and how things just didn't seem to work out for her.

"Huh?" I asked, snapping out of it.

Ms. Gladstone repeated herself, "I can't believe that girl's mother brought Denise and her brother in today."

"Yeah, that is a little strange."

"Her brother didn't stay, though. He went back home with his mother, but Denise is here."

"She seems like she is taking it pretty well," I blurted out to see what Ms. Gladstone thought about Denise's mood.

"Yeah, but you know, Mr. Williams, everyone has their ways of dealing with hard times," she reminded me.

"You're right, Ms. Gladstone," I said. "Well, I have to get going. I have to meet the school psychologist and some of the crisis team members down on the first floor in Ms. Cotton's room to talk to the children."

"All right, Mr. Williams, thank you for coming by."

I got to Ms. Cotton's room five minutes early; the team was already there. Ms. Cotton was standing outside answering their questions.

"Hey, Ms. Cotton, how have you been?" I asked, putting my arm around her.

"Oh, I'm fine, Mr. Williams. Everything is fine. I'm trying to take everything in stride." It was easy to see that she was having a hard time with the situation; she looked a little nervous. She kept peeking her head in and out of the room while she entertained the barrage of questions about Kyree.

When it was time for us to split up and go to our assigned rooms to address the students directly, Jerry stopped me in the hallway. While everyone else went to their rooms, he gave me the play-by-play commentary of the speech in Ms. Cotton's room.

"Williams, this is bullshit. These people don't really care about these kids," he whispered. "Look at the school psychologist. He's just addressing the class because we were fooled in the office, and we think it is a formality. We all think we are following procedure because Mr. Stevens said this technique was used at some school in the suburbs. A grievance center? Please. If these kids are in need of help, let the teacher send the ones that look distressed up to your office to talk. Have the teacher keep an eye out, don't tell the whole class that there will be a grievance center open all day. They'll just use it as a place to cut class and fool around. This kid's death is going to turn into a joke. It was a horrible move on Mrs. Matthews's part to let this happen this way. Boy I tell you, that principal—"

"I know, I know," I said

"She needs to get it together," he continued. "She only agreed with that guy because she didn't want to come across as incompetent. She is acting out of fear. She knows these kids better than he does, and I know her initial reaction would have been to make an announcement on the loud speaker and send a letter home with each child."

While Jerry and I stood in the doorway listening, the school psychologist spoke to the class: "Hello, class. Kyree Jenkins has passed. We have been told that he died last night."

"How did he die?" one of the children asked.

"Uh—uh—he died in his sleep," Rick, the school psychologist, answered nervously.

I could tell he was uncomfortable addressing the class about the issue. He was sweating, and every chance he got, he would glance over at Jerry and me to make sure he was saying the right things.

"See, I told you. This is all wrong. Look how uptight he looks. He keeps looking over here at you and me like we're the psychologists," Jerry whispered as he rolled his eyes.

"If you have any questions, or if you need a place to go, Mr. Williams, our counselor, and Mr. Dan King, an outside counselor, will be in room 108 all day tomorrow. Does anyone have any questions?"

After Rick finished his speech, the room was at a standstill – dead silent. Some children smirked, while some children wore blank expressions. Most of them were looking around the room trying to see what the mood was like. Then it happened: One girl started crying. She was supposed to have been Kyree's girlfriend. As she cried with her head down, a girl next to her started to pat her on the back, and Ms. Cotton walked over to her, rubbing her hands and nodding her head.

The next thing you know, other kids started putting their heads down, and some of them started crying. Some of them were still smirking, and some of them were peeking through their hands to see if anyone was coming over to console them.

"She should've made the announcement on the damn loud speaker," Rick whispered to Jerry and me as he stormed through the doorway back to the office.

"Now he says something. In the meeting, he just sat there like he was constipated, along with everyone else. Oh well, that's how it usually is. Shit just happens, and no one does anything." Jerry spoke for the both of us.

The Next Day in the Grievance Center

Dan and I were not looking forward to working the grievance center, but it was my duty as the guidance counselor and Dan's job as the visiting counselor.

The first guest to come in was Kamary Brown: "What's up, Mr. Williams?"

"How are you feeling, son?"

"Not too good. It's rough, man. I can't believe this is happening."

"I know. It's a very rough time in all our lives. Do you know Mr. King?"

"Mr. King?" Kamary asked, frowning up his face.

"You guys probably know him better as Mr. Dan. He works with some of you from time to time."

"Yeah, I've seen him around."

"Well, look, Kamary, Mr. Dan and I are going to help you get through this situation the best way possible. Is there anything you want to talk to us about?"

"Nah. I just can't be in class. It's hard to do work. Hard for me to concentrate and stuff."

"Well, that's why we are here to help you out and all."

"How well did you and Kyree know each other?" Dan interjected.

"We were cool. We were almost best friends, but Ron had that title."

"Did Ron come to school today?"

"Nah. He didn't come to school, Mr. Williams."

"Do you think he knows about what happened?" I asked right away.

"I don't think so. He wouldn't have any way of knowing because he wasn't in school yesterday, either."

"You don't think he could have gone over to his house and found out?" Dan asked eagerly.

"He didn't really go over there like that. We would all hang out different places."

"What places?" Dan interrupted.

Kamary looked at me. The expression on his face said 'I ain't about to tell this unfamiliar white guy any information and be labeled a snitch.'

I just shook my head and looked at the ground. Although I knew where the kids usually hung out, I knew that Kamary would never open his mouth. He might if it was just him and me talking, but Dan was too much of a stranger.

Before we could finish with Kamary, four more kids were at the door of 108. Within minutes, we had around 23 students in the grievance lounge, including Brian Spence, the worst behaved kid in the sixth grade. We had to be professional. We couldn't turn anyone away from the lounge. Although I knew Spence was in the room for the sole purpose of getting out of class, I treated him like everyone else.

"All right, there are a lot of you in the room now, so let's try to do something in honor of Kyree," I said, expecting full cooperation from everyone. Two women from Dan's agency brought in paper and markers, and everyone quieted.

"What's this for, Mr. Williams?" Brian asked, afraid I was going to have them do a strenuous project. Most of the class was thinking like him, and they showed it with the expressions on their faces.

"Look guys, don't worry. It's not work. We are going to show our love and respect for Kyree. We are going to make cards. You can hand them in to us, keep them, or send them to his family's house. The choice is yours. This process may help some of you deal with the situation a little bit better."

"Aw, bet. I'm going to make a hype card."

"Yeah, that's what's up."

They were off to work. Brian Spence was on his best behavior, and Kamary was taking the assignment very seriously.

A few minutes had passed when Kamary came up to me and asked what I thought about his card. I was impressed. He was very creative, and I could tell from his drawing that he was smart. "Kamary, this is a spectacular card. Kyree would be proud," I said.

"Yeah, you know, I tried to throw down for him, you know?" While Kamary was talking with me, the group began to get a little restless. They started talking, giggling, and fooling around.

"Hey, come on guys. Keep the noise level down. If you're done, you have five more minutes until lunch, and then you can go eat," Dan said, a little annoyed.

"Hey, Mr. Williams, half these guys in here didn't even know Kyree like that. They don't even care. They are just here so they can get out of class," Kamary told me, leaning in close so no one else could hear him. I was not surprised by what he said, but I was surprised that he said it in a room full of his peers, where snitching was forbidden.

"Yeah, you know what, you guys start getting ready for lunch. More than half of you are done and are just fooling around." I knew by saying this, half of them, if not all, would forget about the grievance center and continue on with the rest of their day – all except Kamary.

"Mr. Williams. I'm coming back after lunch. Is that okay?" Kamary asked.

"Yeah, you can come back if you need to."

The sixth graders' lunch was from 11:00 a.m. to noon. Kamary came back to the grievance center around 1:00 p.m. "I thought you were coming back at noon, man."

"I went to gym." Dan and I looked at each other and made facial expressions that said he just might be one of those kids trying to take advantage of the grievance lounge.

Kamary must have picked up on our vibe. "Man, I went to the gym to blow off some steam, but I can't sit in class, though.

It's too hard to concentrate on work," he said as he sat down in a chair and folded his arms.

"Do you want to keep the card you made?" I asked Kamary.

"No, you keep it." He paused. "As a matter of fact, I will take it, and I'll take it to his mother." Kamary reached his hand out for the card.

"That's a nice thought," Dan added.

All of a sudden, we heard a loud knock on the door. All three of us turned to see who it was, and Officer Caroll's frowning face was peeking through the glass. Dan opened the door, and she came storming in with an attitude.

"This is fucking bullshit, man," she said as she stomped over to the coffee table to pick up her charging walkie talkie.

"Come on, Ms. Caroll, watch your mouth. There is a kid in here," I scolded her.

"How you gonna tell me how to talk in my office?"

"Right now, it's not your office; it's the grievance center where these students are coming in for help dealing with Kyree's death."

"Matthews should've used your office for this shit."

"Caroll, you know what? You're an evil woman. You got problems. You need a psychologist." Caroll looked at me sternly, and after a few seconds, she burst out laughing.

She reached to put her hand on my shoulder, and I flinched. "You know what, Williams, I'm trippin.' I'm just having a bad day," she chuckled. "Y'all take it easy. The office is all yours," she said leaving, squeezing her wide body through the narrow opening of the door.

"I'll be right back," Dan said as he left the room. While Dan was gone, Kamary decided to complicate things.

"Mr. Williams, do you think Kyree really hung himself?" Kamary asked, catching me off guard.

"Why do you ask that?" I quickly replied.

"I mean his family wasn't right, and he was going through problems." Before I could ask what kind of problems, Dan walked back into the room, and the expression on Kamary's face told me that he wanted to keep the conversation confidential.

It was going on 2:00 p.m., and I hadn't gone to the bathroom all day. "I'll be back," I said. As I walked to the restroom, I thought about the point Kamary was making. The thought had crossed my mind that Kyree could have been murdered, especially after finding out more about him. He wasn't depressed. He was pretty popular among the sixth graders, and he was outgoing. If this was a suicide, it happened all of a sudden. People say that's how a lot of suicides happen, but something was telling me in my heart that this was no suicide. On my walk back to the lounge, I saw Denise. "Hey, Mr. Williams," she said with that same smirk on her face.

"Hello, sweetheart. How are you holding up?" I asked walking in the opposite direction, getting the sense that she didn't want to stop and talk.

"I'm all right," she said as she went around the corner of the hallway. During my last steps towards the lounge, I thought about how strange it was that she was in school, and even stranger that she had been in school yesterday, the same day the suicide occurred. Denise didn't come into the grievance center all day, nor did her big brother. It was somewhat understandable. I guess they wanted to go to class, as if everything was normal, instead of coming to the center for help and being bombarded with questions.

When I came into the office, Dan had his bag on his shoulder; he was all ready to go. "You leaving?" I asked. "It's only two."

"It's slow in here now that those kids have gone. I have to go to this kid's house and make sure he has a legitimate reason why he didn't come to school today."

"All right, boss. Do your social service."

"Later. I'll talk to you next week to find out how everything went. I won't be in tomorrow."

"Later," I said as Dan left the room. Kamary looked like he wanted to start talking again. Before I could ask him anything, he started where we left off.

"He had problems at home. He didn't get along with his mom like that."

"Did he tell you that? Did he actually say he didn't get along with his mother?"

"Not really, it was just a known fact. Everyone knew that he didn't get along with his mother, but that wasn't his only problem. His sister hated him, too. She's crazy."

"Denise?"

"Yeah."

"What about Kyree's older brother?" I asked.

"Mike? Mike is crazy. They had their times when they didn't get along, but his real problem was his mother and Denise. Mike is older, but Denise bosses everybody around."

"How do you know all this?"

"Just from talking to Kyree, but I also saw it when they would run into each other in the hallway."

"What did you see?"

"Denise would come down to the sixth grade floor and tell Kyree to do something. Kyree would be like he ain't doin' it, but when she came across Mike in the hallway and told him to do something, he would. It would be in a threatening way, too, Mr. Williams. It wasn't nice."

"You've seen her do that?"

"Yeah, everyone has. She broadies both of them. When Kyree didn't do what she wanted, she would beat him up. I mean, I didn't see her do anything, but they would fight. She was so mean, they made her live with her grandmother. The mother's on drugs, and when her and Denise got together, they would gang up on the brothers."

"Wow," I said softly.

"That's why I don't think Kyree killed himself."

"What?"

"I don't think Kyree killed himself. I think his mother or sister did it."

"Look, Kamary, I know this is a hard time, but you can't say things like that. We can only go on what we know and what we were told."

"Yeah, but how is Kyree found at two or three in the morning? Dead! It doesn't make any sense."

"I don't know, son. I don't know." As I sat there with my hand on my forehead, wishing that Kamary would change the topic and stop playing detective, I realized how smart he was.

While I thought, Kamary stared out the window. "You okay?" I asked him.

"Yeah."

"You think you're about ready to head back to class now?"

"What time is it?"

"It's around three, a little bit before."

"Yeah, I can go sit in class for a period." Kamary gave me a hug before he left. "I'm going to find out what happened, Mr. Williams."

"Yeah, okay, Sherlock. Just be careful, and take it easy. If anything else happened that we don't know about, I'm sure the police will take care of it."

He looked at me, sighed, and nodded his head. He should have just said, 'Yeah right.' Many of the children had a hard time believing that someone was going to help them, especially the police, because of what they see in the neighborhood on a daily basis.

Kamary left, and I gathered up all the cards, including his, which he had left behind. Once I had the room clean, I went upstairs to my office to reflect on everything that had happened. Not just the recent incident, but the whole year – so much negativity in so little time. What were we accomplishing?

As I looked through the glass doors of the eighth grade hallway, Denise caught my eye. She was heading to one of the classrooms near the staircase; I stopped to see what she was doing. She banged on the door and told the teacher she needed to speak to Mike. The teacher, who was very rambunctious and often cursed at students who disrespected him, let this one slide because he knew about Denise's situation. When Mike came to the door, he stepped out into the hallway, and closed it – a mindless look on his face. I could see and hear them, but they couldn't see me.

"Daddy wants to hold an investigation," Denise said.

"What?"

"Yeah. I think he knows about what we did to Kyree."

I walked up the stairs when I heard this. I didn't want to hear anymore. It was too scary. That confirmation coming from Denise's very own lips was enough for me.

Once I made it to my office chair, I sat down and tried to convince myself that I did not just hear what I thought I did. I was once concerned about that girl being harassed and getting punched in the face. Now, I sat in denial, trying to convince myself that she didn't murder her younger brother and force her older brother to be an accomplice.

I never told anyone what I heard. I was drained and tired of being part of a system that opened its doors for children to come in and self-destruct. There was never a positive outcome. I did not want to be responsible for two more children getting into a heap of trouble they couldn't get out of. After all I had experienced at Parish Hill, perhaps even I had reached the point where I didn't want to snitch.

It wasn't until that moment that I understood everyone's frustration. "Don't snitch" didn't come from trying to be tough or trying to be a gangster—it came from years of asking for help and getting nothing in return. This attitude of apathy was transferred to children from the adults in their lives and carried into Parish Hill.

The students and teachers had reached the point of putting their hands in the air, and they didn't care what happened, just as long as they made it from one day to the next. The staff was there to get paid, and the students were there to do whatever they wanted. The parents occasionally came to embarrass their children and to blame the school for the wrongs their children suffered. Nothing was ever accomplished. But no one even talked about that.

No one outside of Parish Hill would ever know about the poison that was spreading, because in the streets surrounding the school, and the hallways within it, snitching was forbidden.

Years Later

That is how my year as a substitute guidance counselor at the worst middle school in the city went. It was confusing, frustrating, nerve-wracking, dangerous, and, at times, humorous. I am sure that most of the students would agree with my description and would probably have a few more adjectives to add to the list. I would say that the staff would agree, but most of them would say that Parish Hill is not *that* bad. They do not want to be held accountable for the school's problems. In fact, when I would ask them how they felt about the school, they would say that although it could be better, there were a lot of worse schools out there.

I never returned to Parish Hill to see if staff attitudes had changed, but Willy and Travis kept me up-to-date on the latest failures as I continued my journey, substituting at other inner city middle schools. Dangerous incidents were still happening frequently and most were still going unreported.

My other experiences showed me that, to my surprise, Parish Hill staff was right. Some of the schools were just as bad as

Parish Hill. Saying they were worse would be a bit of a stretch, but just as at Parish hill, incidents happened at those schools that should have been reported and exposed for the whole country to see - but they were not.

Years after my experiences at Parish Hill, I read an article in the *Daily News* that shed some new light on the situation: "State's 25 Most Dangerous Schools All in Phila.," Dafney Tales, August 28, 2009. It contained an updated list of Pennsylvania's 25 most dangerous schools. All of the schools were located in Philadelphia.

The list ranked schools based on the total number of "dangerous incidents" that happened at the school during the past school year. The total number of incidents was compared to the number of students attending the school to determine if the school was dangerous compared to other schools in the state. I was disturbed that 10 new schools had been added to the list in one year's time and that all of the schools were located in Philadelphia, but I was even more disturbed by the definition the state was using to determine what constituted a dangerous incident.

According to the article, Pennsylvania defined a dangerous incident as "one in which weapons possessions or violence results in an arrest." Further investigation revealed that the definition had been in place for at least six years and was in place during my time at Parish Hill. To my disappointment, many of the things I experienced at Parish Hill would not qualify as dangerous under that definition. A student holding a teacher hostage, a child punching another child in the face, a teacher selling bootleg merchandise to students, and an auditorium full of discarded weapons did not result in any arrests (as far as I know), but that did not make them any less dangerous.

Aside from this definition, there was already a perception amongst school administration, staff, and students that telling law enforcement about problems in the school was useless. Like many of the city's residents, those of us inside the school felt that snitching on students and staff by reporting dangerous incidents to outside officials was unlikely to solve any problems: incidents would still occur and there may be some retaliation against those who reported the problems.

The state's definition only created additional incentives for members of school administration to avoid reporting dangerous events to law enforcement. By reporting more dangerous events, administration members increased the likelihood that their school would be labeled one of the most dangerous in the state. No one would help them make the school better, and they might lose their jobs because their schools were not improving or were getting worse.

From what I observed, staff who did not report dangerous events often lost their jobs anyway. Shortly after I left Parish Hill, Principal Matthews was removed and replaced by another principal. Still, overall, it seemed that staff and administration determined that the potential loss from reporting dangerous events outweighed the potential benefit.

By remaining silent, staff and administration strayed from the ultimate goal of developing a secure educational environment for the students. Reporting dangerous events may not have created an immediate benefit, but neither did staying silent. It only made the situation worse by hiding the true depth of the problem. Speaking out about dangerous events and being truthful about their constant presence in our urban institutions is an essential first step towards creating a safe educational environment.

If more school administration, staff, and community members unite in this approach, we can begin turning our public urban institutions into respectable schools. Once this happens, we will see that, ultimately, the gains for everyone outweigh the losses. It is my hope that *Come on Philly* is one of many first steps towards this goal.

The End

www.ingramcontent.com/pod-product-compliance
Lightning Source LLC
Chambersburg PA
CBHW070504100426
42743CB00010B/1759